Better Homes and Gardens®

Decks

YOUR GUIDE TO DESIGNING AND BUILDING

BETTER HOMES AND GARDENS® BOOKS

Des Moines, Iowa

BETTER HOMES AND GARDENS® BOOKS
An Imprint of Meredith® Books

Decks: Your Guide to Designing and Building
Writer: Joe Carter
Editor: Benjamin W. Allen
Associate Art Director: Lynda Haupert
Copy Chief: Angela K. Renkoski
Electronic Production Coordinator: Paula Forest
Production Manager: Douglas Johnston

Editor-in-Chief: James D. Blume
Director, New Product Development: Ray Wolf
Managing Editor: Christopher Cavanaugh

Meredith Publishing Group
President, Publishing Group: Christopher Little
Vice President and Publishing Director: John P. Loughlin

Meredith Corporation
Chairman of the Board and Chief Executive Officer: Jack D. Rehm
President and Chief Operating Officer: William T. Kerr

Chairman of the Executive Committee: E. T. Meredith III

Cover photograph: This elevated deck is shown on pages 7 and 10.

All of us at Better Homes and Gardens® Books are dedicated to providing you with information and ideas you need to enhance your home. We welcome your comments and suggestions about this book on decks. Write to us at: Better Homes and Gardens® Books, Do-It-Yourself Editorial Department, RW-240, 1716 Locust St., Des Moines, IA 50309–3023.

If you would like to order additional copies of any of our books, call 800/678-2803 or check with your local bookstore.

Photographs courtesy of:
Archadeck: 19. California Redwood Association: 18, 74, 75, 86. Crandall & Crandall: 10 (top), 13 (top), 14, 15, 48, 54, 72 (bottom right), 77 (left), 78 (bottom), 84 (bottom), 84 (top), 101, 103. Derek Fell: 44, 68 (top), 69 (bottom). Georgia-Pacific Corporation: 70 (top), 73 (bottom), 85. Julie Maris/Semel: 9, 72 (bottom left), 82, 83, 100. Melabee Miller: 22, 23, 24, 25, 71. Mobil Chemical Company: 33 (top). Bradley Olman: cover, 6, 10 (bottom), 73 (top). Robert Perron: 16, 17, 47, 79. Southern Forest Products Association: 26, 42, 88. Jessie Walker and Associates: 20, 21. Western Wood Products Association: 33 (bottom). Hickson Corporation, producers of Wolmanized wood: 4, 13 (bottom), 78 (top), 80, 81 (bottom).

Deck Design
Sieglinde Anderson: 9. Blair Ballard and Associates: 84 (bottom). Robert Chestnut and Associates, 78 (bottom). Steve Costigan: 70 (top). DeckDesign: 48, 77 (left), 101. Environmental Creations, Inc.: 84 (top). Charles E. Godfrey and Associates: 54. John Herbert Jr. and Associates: 103. Michael Kelly: 10 (top), 72 (bottom right). Robert Knight: 16-17, 17 (top), 17 (bottom), 47, 79. Joey Rusignola: 22, 23, 24-25, 25.

Contents

Introduction

Decks are now considered part of a home's living space even though they are outside. As a room addition, a deck must integrate with your house and yard, and must be legal with regard to local building codes and ordinances. Not only will you need to decide on the size, type, and style of deck you want, but you'll also want to consider access to the house and yard, how much privacy you'd like, and what built-in details, such as benches, you'll need. But don't worry. Although it may sound complex, thorough planning is easier than you might imagine.

Besides the added living space a deck provides during the warm months, these outdoor rooms translate into greater resale value for your home. In fact, if you build the deck yourself, the increase in your home's worth will be much more than you spend on materials.

Decks can be built by do-it-yourselfers with even basic carpentry skills. For those with intermediate skills, only time and effort stand in the way of designing and building a dream deck. That's what *Decks: Your Guide to Designing and Building* is for; it will help you decide what kind of deck is right for you, help you create the design, show you how to buy the right materials, and guide you through the process so you can build a deck that fits your dreams.

How to Use This Guide

Decks: Your Guide to Designing and Building leads you through the process of planning and building a deck. After completing all the phases of this book, you'll be well-armed to develop custom plans for your own deck and know how to turn those plans into reality.

Developing a deck design is an exercise in revision, and the care taken in planning will go a long way toward making your deck the one you want. You should go through the book from cover to cover so you can consider all the factors involved before plunging into your deck project.

Now you're ready to take the first step, learning enough about decks so you can make and execute a plan for success.

Phase One:

"What Kind of Deck?" introduces you to the basic types of decks you might consider and provides a taste of the special features you can build.

"Great Deck Ideas" showcases a gallery of six decks and tells you why these decks met the needs of the homeowners who built them. Photographs also detail specific features that transform these decks from ordinary platforms to things of beauty.

◄ *Simple shade structures, decorative railings, and lattice work are all easy to build and add interest.*

Phase Two:

"All About Materials" spells out your options for everything from concrete and lumber to fasteners. It also shows you how to size lumber correctly, work up a complete shopping list, and set a reasonable budget.

Phase Three:

"Planning and Design" takes you through all the factors you should consider when developing your design and shows you how to get it all down on paper. Along the way, you'll also learn how to obtain permits and follow regulations regarding adding a deck to your home.

"Special Features" shows you how to customize your deck with built-in features such as benches, tables, privacy screens, and shade structures. Plus you'll see how to accommodate a hot tub, outdoor cooking, night lighting, and more. You'll also find some tips on landscaping the perimeter to soften the deck's visual impact.

Phase Four:

"Building Your Deck" gives you the specifics about construction. You'll learn proper techniques for drawing up accurate plans and laying out the site. Then you'll page through all the basics of deck building. You'll discover that most decks, except those that cover steep, inhospitable terrain, are simple structures to build.

What Kind of Deck?

PHASE 1: The first phase of any construction project is to familiarize yourself with your options.

Basics

Decks can range from a small, humble platform at ground level to a truly stunning multitiered deck with running water, sound systems, and lighting. Your deck must not only meet your personal preferences and needs, but also must conform to your house, the surrounding landscape, and the codes applied to your lot. However, before you leap into the decision-making process (more about that in Phase 3), take some time to learn about the basic kinds of decks.

Decks differ in how they are built. They are either attached to the house or are remote. Height, another way decks vary, often indicates the level of building complexity. In order of height and complexity, the kinds of decks are: grade-level, elevated, multi-level, and rooftop decks.

Keep in mind that complexity of decks doesn't end with how they are built or how high they're going to be. Special features add to complexity, but they also add to the livability of any deck, so you may want to keep them in mind as you look at decks. On pages 12 and 13, we've included just a smattering of features to get you thinking about the possibilities as you read the book.

continued

➤ *Although this deck may appear complex, it requires no more carpentry skills than does a standard rectangular deck. Different levels and non-traditional angles make the deck stand out visually.*

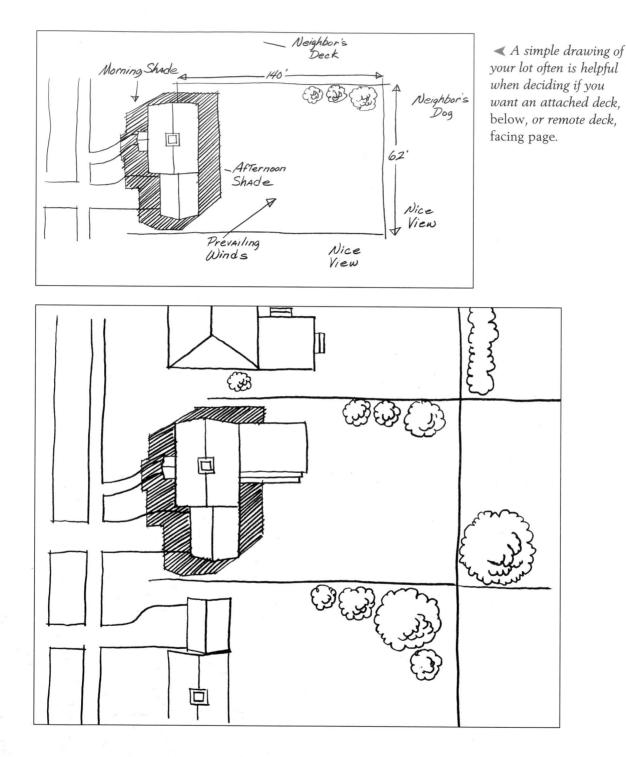

A simple drawing of your lot often is helpful when deciding if you want an attached deck, below, or remote deck, facing page.

The Attached Deck

Easily the most common type, the attached deck is raised off the ground and connected to one or more of the exterior walls of the house, just below the threshold of a door. The attached deck can be a bit easier to build because it requires fewer ground supports and no railing on one side.

More important, however, is its convenience. The deck's direct connection to the house provides easy access and makes it easier to carry food and other items back and forth for entertaining.

But if the aim is to keep deck activities and noise away from the house, the proximity of an attached deck can be a disadvantage.

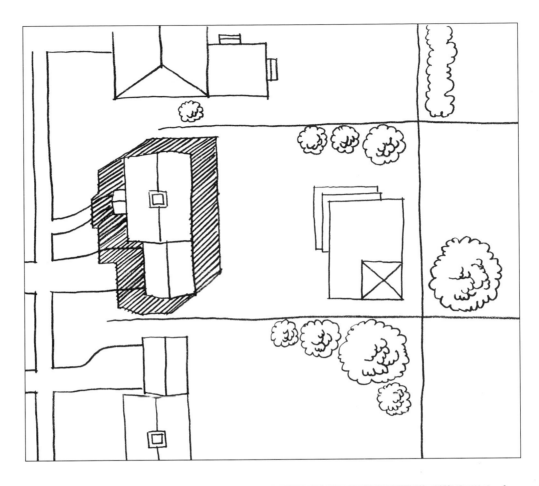

The Remote Deck

As its name implies, a remote deck stands alone and may be well away from the house. In its simplest form a remote deck is a freestanding platform. Stairs, railings, and other features may be desirable depending on the site, but they are not absolutely necessary.

Remote decks can offer more placement choices, especially on larger lots. You might consider a remote deck if a site away from the house is more protected from the neighbors or offers nicer views and better sun or shade.

When it's sufficiently removed, a remote deck also can be more independent of the style of the house. These advantages may outweigh a remote deck's biggest disadvantage—the extra, often inconvenient, steps required to reach it. Such a trip can be eased with a formal walkway to keep the morning or evening dew from soaking shocs.

▲ *Freestanding remote decks allow you to get the view you want.*

Height and Complexity

▲ *A simple grade-level deck can transform a shady area where grass doesn't grow into an outdoor play area; it also requires much less maintenance.*

▲ *The structure below this complex-looking, elevated deck is the same as any easily built deck—simple post-and-beam construction.*

Grade-Level Decks

Built flush with, or one step above, the ground, a grade-level deck is basically a wooden patio. It is usually the simplest to build and accommodates planters and built-in benches. Attached grade-level decks work well with homes that have ground-level access.

A remote grade-level deck can be a perfect retreat from a busy household. It can be designed for many uses from yard games to quiet lounging. It can lie along the edge of an ornamental garden, surround a pool, or support a built-in bench that wraps around the trunk of a favorite shade tree.

Construction is relatively easy, since no support posts or beams are necessary. The support structure of grade-level decks generally rests directly on footings or piers below.

Elevated Decks

An elevated deck stands on posts of any length—12 inches to 12 feet or higher—to reach the main level of the house and/or to flatten a sloping site. Split-level and other house designs with elevated floors put traditional masonry patios too far below indoor living spaces. A deck can solve this problem, just as it can be a solution to the difficulties presented by sloping ground, which often is expensive or impractical to flatten or terrace.

Fortunately, a deck can rise to nearly any height, so it can reach a second story or higher. For example, an elevated design can provide a private sun deck off an upstairs bedroom and be connected to the room with a new door.

Posts, beams, and joists of raised decks make them more complicated to build than grade-level decks. Without extreme heights or steep slopes, building an elevated deck requires nothing more than basic carpentry. If the deck must be very high or the site is particularly steep, professional expertise may be necessary.

▲ *Although the multilevel deck may look complex, simple design can make building one no more complex than four, single-level decks placed close together.*

Multilevel Decks

Multilevel decks provide varying perspectives and allow abundant design possibilities. Whether attached or freestanding, this type of design can serve a number of functions.

■ It helps break up the expanse and possible monotony of a large deck.

■ It defines activity areas separate from the main outdoor living area, such as a play area for children or a dining zone near the kitchen.

■ It resolves the problems presented by a steep slope. Instead of using long posts, the deck has multiple levels that step down or up the hill and more closely follow the land.

Two-level decks are the most common type, but nothing about the construction should prevent you from considering more levels. In fact, a multilevel deck can be nothing more than two or three rectangular decks joined together visually, requiring no structural link. Multilevel decks generally look best when one platform is clearly larger than the other.

Much depends on the topography of the site. The more complex a design, the more desirable the help of a professional designer will be. Steeply sloping sites may require special engineering to meet local codes.

Rooftop Decks

If you lack the land for a deck, or if you simply want a deck as high as your house, consider a rooftop deck. This would only be a do-it-yourself project for those with advanced skills. Roofs, even flat ones, usually aren't made to carry the additional weight of a deck, so initially there are difficult, expensive structural problems to solve.

A common approach is to take off the roof of an attached garage and build a deck over a new flat roof, with access provided by a doorway from a second-story room. The structure of roofs of houses with flat or slightly sloping roofs, however, may not be sufficient support for a deck. Solving these issues requires a structural engineer.

Special Features

Pools and Spas

A deck can fulfill special functions, such as being a surround for a hot tub or swimming pool, which will add comfort and safety, and stand up to years of wet conditions. A pool or hot-tub surround easily can be part of a larger deck complex. For example, a hot-tub surround can be separated from the rest of a deck by a level change or privacy wall.

◄ *The step and a short wood skirt around the hot tub raise the deck so the hot tub can rest on the ground, making installation easier.*

Kitchens

If you plan to do a lot of outdoor cooking, you might want to make part of your deck into an outdoor kitchen. This is an increasingly popular feature, especially in climates with long spans of warm weather.

You can set yourself up in a shady spot with counter space and storage, a sink with running water, a small refrigerator, a gas- or charcoal-fired cooktop and grill, or even a gas oven. When winter comes, the kitchen area can be enclosed by folding doors.

◄ *Changing a railing into an extra-wide storage area allows the addition of an outdoor kitchen without requiring an oversize deck.*

Greenery

Are there trees where you want decking? No problem. Deck design is flexible; both structural members and deck boards easily can detour around any trunk. Call it a tree surround and make it a distinctive feature. The trunk also can serve as the center of other features, such as a built-in planter or a built-in bench. You don't need a tree to add features like these. Built-in benches, planters, and tables can be distinctive features of any deck.

Shade Structures

For sites overexposed to the sun, consider a shade structure that's both practical and elegant. These simple structures use tilted boards to block the sun while maintaining ventilation, and they double as leafy vine arbors that provide a lush, cooling canopy. In addition, a structure with the right lumber and/or vegetation, such as a deck fence or a trellis for perennial or annual climbers, provides adequate privacy.

➤ *Don't let a tree inhibit the design of your deck. Cross-bracing between joists allows you to include your favorite tree and have instant shade.*

➤ *A shade structure can add both privacy and a cool spot at midday.*

PROBLEM **?** SOLUTION

If you don't know where to start when designing a deck, follow these decision-making steps.

1. Decide if the deck will be attached to the house or remote and freestanding. Usually this choice comes down to convenient access as opposed to a great view.

2. Decide if the deck will be grade-level, elevated, or multilevel. If your deck is attached, locate at least one level at the same height as the threshold of the door to the house. The number of levels then probably will be determined by the slope and what uses of the deck you envision.

3. Further modification of design accommodates special features such as pools and spas, outdoor kitchens, trees, or shade structures.

◄ Consider your screens carefully. The screen in this seating area blocks the view of the street below without blocking sunlight.

Great Deck Ideas

Take a look at these prime examples of great decks to start getting ideas for your own.

Great decks need not be architectural marvels that only an engineer could design and build. What makes a deck great has more to do with how it works for the people using it and how well it fits into the design of the house or area surrounding it. Oftentimes a deck stands out for the simple reason that it transforms the outdoors into a serene spot to enjoy a wonderful sunset, a sunny day, or a cool evening.

Up in the Air

When the yard is really just a steep slope, a deck can be the only way to have some usable outdoor living space. Perched high on stilt-like posts, this small deck, *right*, provides what the lay of the land could not. Connected back to the hill by a short ramp, this structure is easily accessible several steps from the house.

Being up among the treetops may afford nice views, but it also puts the deck squarely in the sun, making the shade structure a real necessity. With lattice shielding people from both the overhead and western sun, the deck can be used for more hours in the day.

If you're faced with building on a similarly challenging hillside, you'll probably want to consult with an engineer about the best way to plant and secure long posts. You might even want to farm out the foundation work. After that, this deck, like most others, can be built with standard materials and techniques, except for working at greater heights.

➤ What at first glance may appear to be a complex deck is really just simple features put together wisely. The large size, a shade structure, built-in benches, and lighting combine for maximum use and enjoyment.

Down to Earth

Fitting in with the house and the immediate environment is one thing that decks can do very well given an appropriate design. The low-slung deck of Western red cedar at this seaside home is a perfect example of how a simple design also can be an elegant one. With no railings, posts, or balusters, it doesn't block views from inside the house. The wraparound steps make for a graceful transition from the deck to the ground, which further minimizes the deck's physical presence and lets the landscaping be the focus.

At the right side of the house, instead of squaring off the corner, the architect put in a simple curve, a detail achieved with a bit of extra cutting and bending. The treads are short lengths of curved material cut from wider lumber, and the stair risers are bent to make the steps follow the graceful curved line.

➤ *The graceful curve adds to the deck's appearance of expanse by placing the other end of the deck out of sight around the curve.*

▼ *Built-in benches were not used on this deck so the clean lines wouldn't be interrupted.*

▲ *Deck design can even be modified to accommodate a perfect hammock tree.*

PHASE 1: Great Deck Ideas 17

Waterworks

▲ *One advantage of a pool deck surround made from redwood is that it's cool on your feet compared to a standard concrete apron.*

For pool and hot-tub owners, there's enough maintenance in just taking care of the water. Whatever can eliminate or at least minimize extra work is desirable. That makes using redwood or treated wood a good idea, because redwood can last nearly indefinitely in a frequently wet environment.

A pool or hot-tub surround built as a deck is also an easy way to create more usable living space when the ground slopes down and away from the pool. A deck surround is simple to build over a concrete slab if that's what you have already. If the area around your deck is open ground, you can use footings and piers to support the deck surround.

To ease installation, place the hot tub directly on the ground and use the deck as a platform that is flush with the top of the hot tub, hiding the plumbing on the sides.

➤ *Hot tubs that sit on the ground don't require a stronger structure to hold the weight of the water.*

Private Affair

When the neighbors are close by, people often look for a little privacy in their outdoor living. When space is limited, a deck still can have plenty of features that add both interest and function. The design of this deck, *below*, succeeds in a number of ways. It effectively provides privacy with the stylish lattice screen that doubles as a trellis. The vines also will have a place to grow along the overhead structure and provide more shade and sense of enclosure.

Though the deck is compact, there's still room for a built-in bench and planter, features that add both function and a pleasing appearance. Strengthening the appearance is the matching of the color of the deck with the house siding.

Because of the considerable distance between the ground and the back door, two levels of steps were built. That puts the main activity area several steps below the back door, and thus out of the direct view of the indoor living area. The two-stage design also breaks up what would have been a long run of steps to the yard. Long runs in a small space tend to become too dominant an architectural element.

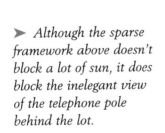

◄ Choose plants that will thrive where you put them. Shade-loving plants, such as impatiens, begonias, and caladium, among others, add color to this small deck.

► Although the sparse framework above doesn't block a lot of sun, it does block the inelegant view of the telephone pole behind the lot.

◄ At the edge of the stairs, alternate steps are deliberately shortened to provide space for plants and flowers.

PHASE 1: Great Deck Ideas **21**

Expansive Living

When your lifestyle calls for lots of space and some special features, the design can respond. Here an expanse of grade-level decking is highlighted in one area with an in-ground hot tub and an elegant overhead structure at one end.

Grade-level designs work best on ground that is already mostly flat or can be made so with slight excavation. When there is more slope than can be reasonably flattened, an additional level should be planned.

For a single-level deck built into an area that's been partially excavated, good drainage under the deck is crucial and should be thoroughly handled before any construction begins. This may involve regrading ground to ensure surface water flows where it should—away from the house or to specific drainage points.

Distinguish activity areas on a large deck by strategic furniture placement, laying decking in different directions, and adding built-in features.

continued

➤ *Natural materials can help a deck ease into the landscape. Rock is used here as the retaining wall, needed after excavating to make room for the deck.*

◄ *Table umbrellas can provide the shade you need until young trees grow to shade the deck.*

▲ *This view shows how the large deck is a number of separate activity areas, with different features marking each area.*

◄ *A shade structure sets off a gardening area, complete with potting bench.*

All About Materials

PHASE 2: The next decisions to make regard types of materials—choices dictated by style and function.

Decks use the basic materials of metal-fastened wood standing on concrete. After the design, your choice of materials will most affect the deck's cost. Knowledge of deck parts, the advantages of different materials and how to choose them, what size lumber you'll need, and how to connect it all should allow you to start picking out what you'll need.

Anatomy of a Deck

Although basic construction is relatively easy (see Phase 4), deck building features some unusual vocabulary when it comes to purchasing materials. The illustration below lists the major parts of a deck and shows its post-and-beam construction. The topmost part is the cap rail over the railings. These are supported by rail posts and usually fastened to joists. Vertical supports called balusters or spindles (not shown in the illustration) stand between the posts. The decking also rests on joists and sometimes

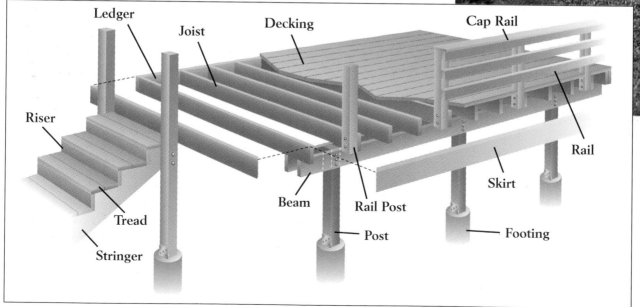

▲ *Most decks are made completely from lumber, but there are choices to be made about what kind to use before construction begins. These choices affect cost, durability, and the final look the lumber will have.*

on beams if the joists and beams are on the same plane. Usually, though, joists sit on beams, which in turn sit on posts. The posts stand on masonry piers resting on concrete footings below ground.

With on-ground decks, the joists and beams sit directly on the piers and footings. Ledgers, which also support joists, connect an attached deck to a house. On some decks the posts extend up through the decking to support the railing. Stairs consist of stringers, which support the horizontal treads and the vertical risers. Many decks have open-stair designs with no risers.

The Right Wood for Decks

Redwood, cedar, bald cypress, and pressure-treated wood are the most common wood types for deck building. The first three resist rot and insects naturally. Pressure-treated lumber is factory-made, with chemicals forced into the wood fibers under extreme heat and pressure. The table below tells more about these species and the advantages and disadvantages of each.

Which Wood?

Redwood

Some lower-cost common-grade redwood is fine for framing members, decking, and railings. Avoid wood with light-colored sapwood, which is not as rot-resistant. Use construction-heart or more expensive clear-heart grades for posts and other near-ground structural members.

Appearance

With its deep red look, redwood can work with many architectural styles. Left unfinished, it weathers to a silvery gray. Preserve its natural color with a clear wood finish or re-create it with a redwood stain. Redwood also accepts any exterior stain color to match house siding or trim.

Cedar

Western red cedar is available in premium, common, and construction grades. (The latter have more knots.) Be sure to get lumber that's surfaced on all sides. As with redwood, avoid sapwood-streaked or surface-void lumber (pecky cedar).

Cedar has an appealing golden brown appearance with a distinctly different look from that of redwood. It will weather to grayish tones, but a clear wood finish will somewhat preserve cedar's natural color.

Durability

Heartwood is all but impervious to rot and insects; the lesser common and construction grades are more vulnerable because they contain sapwood. To prevent mildew in wet climates, apply a penetrating oil sealer or stain.

Uses

You can use redwood for all parts of a deck, but its high cost may convince you to use it for visible parts only, such as decking, railing, and other deck-top built-ins.

Installation

Redwood is relatively soft, so use washers when framing and bolting members together. Space deck boards ⅛ to ¼ inch apart to allow for proper drainage. If you nail near the ends of boards, drill holes to prevent splitting.

Cost

Redwood is the costliest deck material, especially for those who live far from its West Coast source. It is up to four times more expensive than pressure-treated lumber and about twice the price of cedar lumber.

Cedar is equal to redwood in its resistance to rot and pests.

Use cedar generally in nonstructural applications because it's weaker than redwood, cypress, and pressure-treated pine. Its frailty may be a reason to use other lumber for posts, beams, and joists.

Cedar installation is the same as for redwood, although decking should definitely be screwed in place not nailed.

On average, the cost of cedar is about half the price of similar grades of redwood and about twice the cost of pressure-treated lumber, making it a good value.

continued

Which Wood? *continued*

Cypress

Southern cypress (also called bald cypress) comes in common and premium grades. Although its growing region is the Southeast, you can special-order cypress in other regions.

Appearance

Cypress is a reddish tan color, lighter than both redwood and cedar.

Pressure-Treated Wood

Southern pine, and sometimes fir, composes most pressure-treated lumber. Grading is simple: #2 is most common and has some knots; #1 is mostly clear. A clear grade is quite high in price. CCA and ACA designations refer to the treatment process: Check posts for the ground contact rating, which indicates higher treatment pressure.

CCA
Pressure-
Treated
Wood

Pressure-treated lumber has a greenish cast that weathers to gray, with a more pronounced grain than other deck woods. It readily accepts any exterior stain tone.

Durability

Southern cypress is equal to redwood in its resistance to rot and pests.

Uses

You can use cypress in both structural and ornamental applications, but its high cost may warrant generally visible uses in decking, railings, and other deck-top locations.

Installation

Because it's harder than cedar, you can nail down decking rather than screwing it down. Cypress is prone to twisting and warping if not relatively dry when installed. Ask your supplier to confirm a low-moisture content.

Cost

Cypress is least expensive in its own region, but outside of the Southeast the price climbs steeply, at times exceeding redwood costs.

Because of the pressure treatment, this lumber is equal to natural species in its resistance to rot and pests. Make sure you select good pressure-treated wood. Junk wood that's pressure treated will just be junk wood that lasts a long time.

You can build your whole deck with pressure-treated lumber. Another money-saving option is using it for structural underpinnings while using more expensive, and possibly more appealing, decking and railing lumber.

Pressure-treated lumber should dry for at least a couple weeks after delivery. After installation, coat all surfaces with a water-repellent sealer. (Some brands come with the sealer already applied as part of the pressure-treatment process.)

Pressure-treated wood, easily the least expensive deck lumber, is one-fourth to one-half the price of redwood, cedar, or cypress.

Lumber Quality

Whatever wood you choose, check it carefully before you buy it. If you're picking through a pile, reject any twisted, warped, or split pieces, or those with large, loose knots or signs of weakness. Otherwise you'll cope with those problems for years. Also remember that stock wider than 6 inches tends to cup and warp, so keep the deck boards to that size or less (2×6, 2×4, 2×3, and 5⁄4×6). Structural members such as joists and beams often must exceed those sizes; avoid structural lumber with visible problems.

Most wood suitable for deck building will weather to a pleasant, go-with-everything gray. To maintain the tones or change the color, use clear wood finishes or exterior stains, as described on page 108.

You must first decide on all your lumber dimensions (see the tables on pages 34 through 37). Use them to determine the code-approved dimensions for every piece of your deck and to make smarter decisions. For example, save lumber money and digging time by installing a hefty beam instead of numerous posts.

Check out decks completed by friends and neighbors to get a firsthand look at construction details. You'll probably discover a pattern of lumber sizes they used and where they were used in the design. Ask them what they might do differently so you can learn from their mistakes. Also ask what they did well to learn practical lessons.

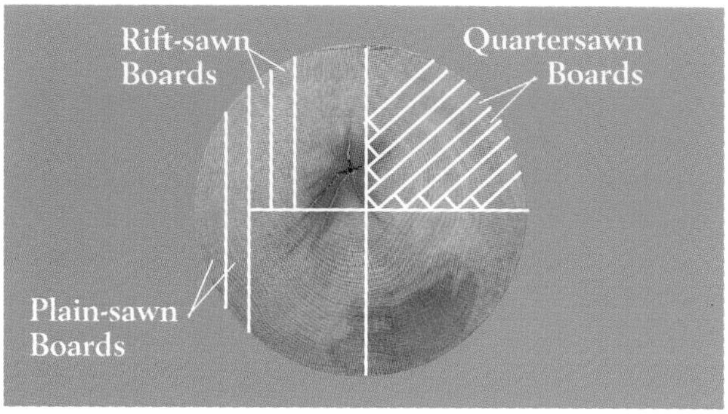

Different cuts from a log produce different types of lumber. Rift-sawn and plain-sawn boards are sometimes susceptible to warping. Most decking is made from rift-sawn or plain-sawn boards. Plain-sawn boards are sometimes called flat-sawn boards. Quartersawn boards, with growth rings at 60° to 90° to the face of the board, are often the most expensive of the three and warp the least of any cut.

When estimating your lumber needs, remember that the actual dimensions are slightly less than common lumber sizes. For example, a 2×4 actually measures 1½×3½ inches. Always figure the actual dimensions of wood you'll be using when you plan and measure, and use nominal dimensions when ordering (see at *left*).

For your own sake list everything you need in a logical order and in detail. (See the sample shopping list on page 39.) For example, if your project calls for 12 pieces of 2×4 exactly 8 feet long, list the items that way.

Nominal and Actual Lumber Dimensions

"Nominal" means what it is labeled. "Actual" are the dimensions you should use when calculating measurements.

Nominal	Actual	Nominal	Actual
1×2	¾×1½"	2×3	1½×2½"
1×3	¾×2½"	2×4	1½×3½"
1×4	¾×3½"	2×6	1½×5½"
1×6	¾×5½"	2×8	1½×7½"
1×8	¾×7¼"	2×10	1½×9¼"
1×10	¾×9½"	2×12	1½×11¼"
1×12	¾×11¼"	4×4	3½×3½"
2×2	1½×1½"	6×6	5½×5½"

THE RIGHT STUFF

Plastic Wood

Landscaping and deck building have entered the realm of recycling, with wood waste and used plastic shopping bags recycled to form plastic lumber. Recycled plastic is combined with sawdust; the resulting mix is extruded into a number of shapes. For example, the Trex brand, made by the Mobil Chemical Company, is available in 1×6, 2×4, $5/4$×6, 2×6, 2×8 and 2×10 standard lumber dimensions.

While not approved for any load-bearing applications (i.e., as a joist or post), Trex offers a suitable alternative for decking, as shown *right*. It also can be used for railings, skirting, and other more decorative uses. You can saw, nail, glue, and otherwise handle Trex just as you would natural wood. In appearance, it starts out as a deep brown tone, but soon weathers to a light tan-gray. It requires no preservative or stain, except where a different appearance is desired. Trex costs about the same as the best grades of redwood or cedar lumber. For more information on Trex, call 800/289-8739.

If you buy pressure-treated lumber, make sure that it is from a reputable source and bears an inspection stamp ensuring the lumber meets the minimum national standards of preservative retention and depth (the amount of preservative and how deeply it's forced into the wood).

It's a good idea to season the lumber so it adjusts to the moisture content of your area. To season it, stack the wood to lie flat in a dry area, loosely covered, and put thin spacers between each layer to promote air circulation. Better grades of redwood, cedar, and cypress usually are kiln-dried and will season quickly. Pressure-treated lumber may need a longer seasoning time. To prevent excessive checking (cracks on the face and ends of a board), coat pressure-treated lumber with a water-repellent sealer soon after it's in place on the deck.

Also remember that outdoors, wide members shrink, swell, and cup more than narrow ones. When you need wide members, such as 2×6 deck planks, choose quartersawn boards with edge- or vertical-grain, as shown *facing page, top right*.

▲ *Western species of wood don't absorb preservatives as well as Southern pine and need a little help. Incised wood has little knife cuts in the face of the wood to help the preservative penetrate the wood. If you're using a Western species that's pressure treated for structural members, they should be incised.*

What Size Lumber?

Deciding the structure of your deck works in exactly the opposite way that you will build it. Generally, you decide by starting at the top and working down. Building starts at the bottom and goes up. By deciding what type decking and keeping in mind the size deck you might want, you set the stage for all other structural members below. Use the Sample Deck on the *facing page* as a guide to the tables of minimum lumber requirements on pages 34 through 37.

Not all species of wood are equally strong or available. Ask your supplier about availability in your area.

Note: These tables assume a live load of 60 pounds per square foot. If your building code permits lighter design loads, permissible spans may be longer or dimensions smaller. Check with your local building department or inspector.

What Grade Decking?

For deck flooring, some lumberyards recommend only #1 lumber. Because the top grade has fewer knots and flaws, it should be less susceptible to warping and twisting. For a 12×12-foot deck, the additional cost between #2 and #1 grades should be less than $20, which is money well spent for the better grade. You'll get fewer problems and have a nicer, more uniform-looking deck.

When referring to the tables for joists, beams, and posts, use the chart *below* to identify the species of wood you're working with. The chart is based on construction-grade lumber or better.

Species Chart

1 Douglas fir, larch, and Southern pine
2 Western red cedar, white fir, pines other than Southern and Eastern, and Sitka spruce
3 Northern and Southern white cedar, balsam fir, and redwood

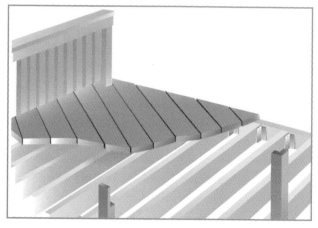

Decking

1. Deck boards. The choice of the species and size of deck board comes first. The type of decking you choose will determine the joist spacing. For example, if you want to economize on redwood decking by using ⁵⁄₄×6s, you'll have to put the joists on 16-inch centers.

1 Allowable Spans for Most Commonly Used Decking

Size of Decking	Allowable Space Between Joists
1×4 or 1×6	16"
2×4 or 2×6	16"
2×4 on edge	24"
Decking Board (1¼" board laid flat)	16"

Sample Deck

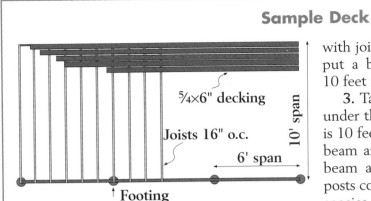

⁵⁄₄×6" decking

Joists 16" o.c.

10' span

6' span

↑ Footing

If you wanted an 8-foot-high, 10×18-foot deck with ⁵⁄₄×6 decking board laid flat, shown *above*, you would use the following steps to determine the structure to hold it up. Values in the tables that were used are highlighted in yellow.

1. Table 1 shows us the joists need to be 16 inches on center using ⁵⁄₄×6 decking.

2. Because we want to use treated Southern pine, we look at species 1 in Table 2 to find that 2×8 joists can span up to 12 feet, 10 inches

with joists 16 inches apart. This means we can put a beam at the outer edge of our deck, 10 feet from the ledger attached to the house.

3. Table 3 tells us how far apart the posts under the beam need to be. Because our beam is 10 feet from the house (120 inches between beam and ledger), we decide on a 3×10 for a beam and place the posts 6 feet apart. The posts could be 7 feet apart because we're using species 1, but we decided to space the footings equally for visual appeal. It's OK for your spans to be less than what's listed in the tables.

4. Finally we use Table 4 to check the load area the posts can carry. Our beams are 10 feet apart, and we have posts every 6 feet, giving us a load area of 60 (10 multiplied by 6). Table 4 shows that any species of the three sizes of posts shown will hold up the load area. The 4×4s are therefore adequate and are the least expensive size to use.

2. Joists. Joist-spacing choices offer a variety of maximum allowable spans between posts or beams, depending on joist size (2×6, 2×8, etc.) and wood species. Select the span based on total deck size and economical combination of posts and beams. Typically, larger decks require larger joists to minimize posts and footings. For example, with 2×8 pressure-treated Southern pine for joists, there's no beam or post for up to a 12-foot, 10-inch span when placed on 16-inch centers.

2	**Maximum Joist Spans**		
		Joist Spacing	
Species	**Joist Size**	**16"**	**24"**
1	2×6	9'9"	7'11"
	2×8	12'10"	10'6"
	2×10	16'5"	13'4"
2	2×6	8'7"	7'0"
	2×8	11'14"	9'3"
	2×10	14'6"	11'10"
3	2×6	7'9"	6'2"
	2×8	10'2"	8'1"
	2×10	13'0"	10'4"

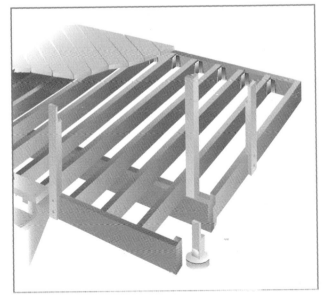

Joists

What Size Lumber?

3. Beams. Large designs may require a beam or two. If so, determine the optimum beam size by choosing a maximum span that divides fairly evenly into the length or width of the deck (whichever is perpendicular to the direction of the joists).

3   **Maximum Beam Spans**

Spacing Between Beams	Beam Size	Allowable Beam Spans Between Posts Species of Wood (see chart)		
		1	2	3
48"	4×6	6'0"	5'10"	5'10"
	3×8	8'10"	7'9"	7'6"
	4×8	10'0"	9'0"	8'2"
	3×10	11'0"	10'4"	9'6"
	4×10	12'0"	11'4"	10'6"
	3×12	13'0"	12'0"	11'4"
	4×12	14'0"	13'0"	12'4"
60"	4×6	5'10"	5'8"	5'6"
	3×8	7'6"	7'0"	6'8"
	4×8	9'6"	8'6"	8'0"
	3×10	10'6"	9'8"	9'0"
	4×10	11'4"	10'4"	9'10"
	3×12	12'4"	11'4"	10'6"
	4×12	13'6"	12'6"	12'0"
72"	4×6	5'6"	5'5"	5'2"
	3×8	7'0"	6'6"	6'2"
	4×8	9'0"	8'2"	7'9"
	3×10	10'2"	9'4"	8'9"
	4×10	11'2"	10'2"	9'6"
	3×12	12'0"	11'0"	10'0"
	4×12	13'0"	12'0"	11'6"
84"	4×6	4'0"	4'0"	3'8"
	3×8	6'6"	6'0"	5'10"
	4×8	8'4"	7'10"	7'4"
	3×10	9'8"	9'0"	8'6"
	4×10	11'0"	10'0"	9'2"
	3×12	11'6"	10'6"	10'6"
	4×12	12'6"	11'6"	11'0"
96"	3×8	6'2"	5'10"	5'6"
	4×8	8'0"	7'6"	7'0"
	3×10	9'0"	8'4"	8'0"
	4×10	10'0"	9'4"	8'6"
	3×12	11'6"	10'6"	10'0"
	4×12	12'0"	11'0"	10'6"

continued

3   **Maximum Beam Spans**

Spacing Between Beams	Beam Size	Allowable Beam Spans Between Posts Species of Wood (see chart)		
		1	2	3
108"	4×8	7'0"	6'6"	6'0"
	3×10	8'0"	7'4"	6'10"
	4×10	9'0"	8'4"	7'8"
	3×12	10'0"	9'0"	8'6"
	4×12	10'8"	10'2"	9'6"
120"	4×8	6'0"	5'8"	5'2"
	3×10	7'0"	6'6"	6'0"
	4×10	8'0"	7'4"	6'8"
	3×12	9'0"	8'0"	7'6"
	4×12	10'0"	9'6"	9'0"

4   **Post Sizing**

Load Area Posts Can Carry by Species			Height of Deck
1	2	3	**For 6-Foot-High Decks**
144	144	144	4×4
144	144	144	4×6
144	144	144	6×6
1	2	3	**For 8-Foot-High Decks**
144	132	96	4×4
144	144	144	4×6
144	144	144	6×6
1	2	3	**For 10-Foot-High Decks**
108	84	60	4×4
144	132	96	4×6
144	144	144	6×6
1	2	3	**For 12-Foot-High Decks**
36	-	-	4×4
120	84	60	4×6
144	132	132	6×6

4. Posts. Knowledge of the beam spacing (in feet) and post spacing (in feet, both from the previous tables) allows you to determine post sizes by multiplying those two numbers. For example, for beams 12 feet apart and set over posts 8 feet apart, the "load area" in Table 4 is 96. That means you can use a 4×4 redwood post for up to 8 feet of elevation or a 4×6 for up to 10 feet. Decks raised more than 6 feet require additional post bracing regardless of the post size.

Generally, posts are as wide as the beam resting on them so construction is easier, but check Table 4 to ensure you're using the right size post based on the load area.

When you've figured out all sizes, simply count the number of each piece, as shown on your plans. When ordering your lumber, specify deck board lengths to reduce waste. You may have to buy about 10 percent more to cover any unavoidable waste.

Fasteners and Connectors

Screws and nails

Lag screw and bolts

Lumber connectors

Using the right fasteners is important. Fasteners and connectors must withstand years of exposure and stress without rusting or marring the wood.

When fastening the deck boards, ring- and spiral-shank nails will provide a better grip than the common wood nail. If you're using nails, at a minimum, use galvanized nails to resist rust; in fact, you might want to pay a bit more for stainless-steel ones. Choose galvanized buglehead screws for more holding power, and use a power screwdriver to sink them into the wood. As long as the wood lasts, the screws will never pop up and will reduce the problems of warp-prone or high-moisture lumber.

It's also best to use bolts below the decking, the area that withstands the greatest stress. For the strongest method, you can through-bolt with a machine or carriage bolt, which uses a nut and washer for maximum compression and holding power. The lag screw is almost as strong as a bolt.

Before metal lumber connectors were invented, only the highly skilled could execute mortise-and-tenon and other crafty joints. Average-skilled people now can use quite stable joist hangers, post caps, post anchors, and other ingenious devices instead of having to learn more complex carpentry skills.

If you're attaching your deck to masonry or concrete, you may need a specialized masonry fastener for a secure connection. Look for such sophisticated devices as wedge or sleeve anchors. They're a little more expensive than the common lead shield (used with a lag screw) but are more reliable.

Making a Shopping List

Once you've filled in this shopping list, get competitive bids and broker the entire package. Smart suppliers will offer discounts on their regular retail prices if you buy all or most materials from them. If you don't see a discount, ask for one. If they tell you it's already included, go straight to the bottom line to compare with other suppliers. Look for the lowest price, but also look at a supplier's lumber to ensure its quality. Negotiate how the supplier will deliver the lumber; ask to have the lumber dropped off near your work site to save you hauling time and labor. Also, ask for help and insist on selecting the best pieces.

Item	Quantity	Cost/Unit	Total
Footings			
Concrete			
Gravel			
Piers			
Structure			
Ledger			
Posts			
Beams			
Joists			
Bracing			
Edging			
Visible Lumber			
Decking			
Railing			
Extras such as Benches, Planters, and Visual Screens			
Hardware			
Nails or Screws			
Bolts			
Post Attachments (to Beams and to Footings)			
Joist Attachments			
Finishes			
Preservatives			
Sealers			
Stains or Paint			

▲ *Although serviceable, this plain deck detracts from the look of the house.*

Finalizing Your Design

PHASE 3: Now it's time to consider all the factors influencing your design and put your plan on paper.

Now that you've got some idea of the materials you'll need to use, you're ready to develop your deck's basic design and draw up a plan. Starting with your anticipated uses of the deck, Phase 3 takes you through all the factors that may influence your deck design, including those that have to do with the site you choose, legal considerations, and the all-important budget. As you consider these factors, you'll develop a rough design that works for you and your family, your house, and the site.

Once you've produced your rough design, you move on to committing your final plan to paper. If you're not a skilled artist, don't worry about drawing plans that look great. Just keep your pencil sharp and stay on top of the details. The point of your final plan is to clearly illustrate the deck you're going to build, not be a fancy piece of art to hang on the wall. Remember, the care and attention you give to your final plan will make the difference between a smooth deck raising and one filled with headaches.

➤ *A good plan considers existing structures, too, even old uninspiring decks. The plan for this deck revision was to create a deck compatible with the house. Rails, stairs, landscaping, and color all changed, but the size stayed the same.*

Anticipated Use

Think of your deck as a living area, with furnishings that will influence its size and layout. If you enjoy outdoor cooking, you may wish to build an area for a grill. If you expect to entertain large groups, you may want built-in seating. (See pages 72 and 73 for sizing benches and various pieces of furniture and accessories.)

Go with the high end of your size estimates, since the last thing you want is a cramped deck. Plenty of elbow room represents one of the most basic benefits of outdoor living. Create smaller, more private areas in the deck's design, with seating arrangements, screening elements, multiple levels, and other design devices.

Your anticipated use will affect your deck design and size. However, your lifestyle may change after the deck is built, so look ahead. If what you build is too small for future needs, you won't be satisfied. If you go overboard and end up with too much deck, you're wasting money.

See the tip "How Big?" and the section on size and shape on page 44 for advice on sizing.

Look at your family's lifestyle, and consider the following points.

■ If you just want a basic deck for occasional relaxation, room for snacks, or some reading and resting, you don't need a large deck. The simpler your design is, the easier and cheaper it will be to build.

■ If your family enjoys the outdoors or if you entertain regularly, design a larger deck based on the maximum number of people you anticipate will regularly use it.

■ If you enjoy grilling, design a grilling area separate from other activity zones and traffic routes.

■ If children might use the deck often, consider a separate zone with built-in toy storage.

■ If a hot tub is in your plans, design a more private deck that can hold its weight.

➤ *If you wish to have separate activities on a deck, build areas for them into your design. Here a step and a short screen separate the lounging and reading area from the outdoor dining area.*

▲ *The design lines of most ranch houses are horizontal. This deck was designed with that in mind to match the look of the house.*

Practical Matters

Think compatibility when you consider how your deck will look when you connect it with your house. The architectural style of your house will influence all aspects of your deck's design: size and shape, proximity of the deck (attached or remote), its height (also greatly influenced by the terrain), and access (passage to and from the house). You also should consider details such as trim to match that on the house and the color of the decking.

Proximity

How close to home should your deck be? In Phase 1 we introduced the two basic options—attached and remote—and noted the popularity and convenience of an attached deck. But keep thinking about your choices. For example, if locating your deck in the shade is your greatest concern, a remote deck under trees would best suit your needs in a hot climate.

continued

▲ *Gentle curves are not your only option when customizing the edge of your deck. You may want to notch the decking to enhance the natural terrain.*

Money $ Saver

How Big?

Accurately judging the space you need for your deck will save lumber costs. Your house and lot size—in addition to your intended use—will determine the best size.

For your optimum deck size, estimate the largest number of people likely to occupy your deck. Also decide if you want a lot of big parties or mostly small gatherings. Use the rule-of-thumb of 20 square feet of deck area per person to estimate the total size. If 15 people will occupy your deck at once, then it should be about 300 square feet (10×30 feet or 15×20 feet). This by no means is too large, given your future needs for adjustment, and doesn't preclude parties of 20 or 25 people.

Size and Shape

The size of your deck should be in line with your house. An oversize job will overwhelm the house scale and loom larger than you need. For example, attached decks rarely stand much wider than the house. A deck deeper than the house's front-to-back dimensions may only suit a house in a climate with year-round activity.

Do you want a big square or a rectangle, or would you prefer a deck with five or six sides? One advantage of unusual shapes is that they may harmonize better with your home, yard, and personal tastes. A wood deck lends itself well to a variety of free-form treatments, even curves. Cutting off or angling one or more of the outside corners is a simple modification to a square or rectangular deck, but it adds interest to the deck's design. Using shapes other than the standard rectangle may add some complexity to the structural underpinnings, but the construction techniques are the same.

Style

One area of a deck where you should carefully consider style is the railing. Railings are one of the aspects of decks most visible when standing away from your deck and therefore have a great impact on the look of the deck. Commonly available lumber may look more rustic than your house. If so, you might consider buying treated wood for the railing, even though the decking may be made of redwood, then painting your railings to match the house. If your house has weathered shake siding, by all means buy the redwood for the railings and let it weather to match the house's color. In either case you can make the railing's style match that of the house.

Other elements of style compatibility are color and detail. Avoid an awkward added-on look by staining your deck with a color similar to the house, or, if it's best, preserve the wood's natural color with clear coatings. Transplant trim or other elements of the house to the deck. (A Victorian house will offer many opportunities.)

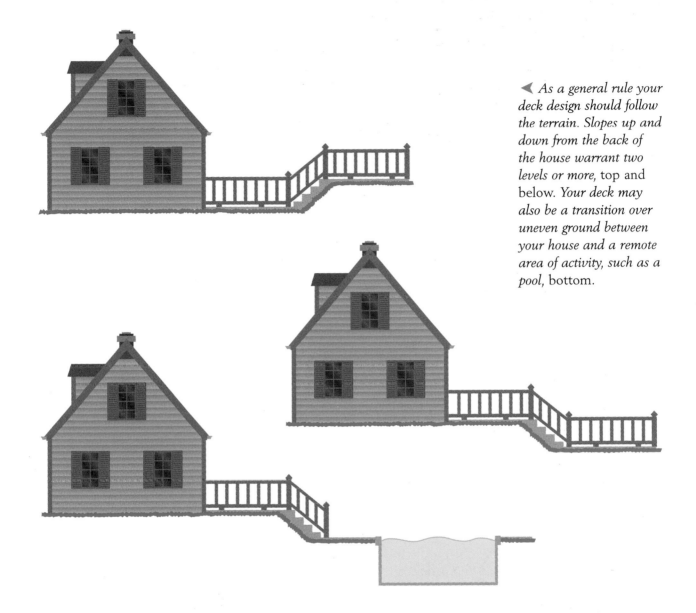

◄ *As a general rule your deck design should follow the terrain. Slopes up and down from the back of the house warrant two levels or more*, top and below. *Your deck may also be a transition over uneven ground between your house and a remote area of activity, such as a pool,* bottom.

Terrain

When you've determined the size of your deck-to-be, either attached or remote, you can see how the lay of your land will affect the design. For example, small to medium decks (up to about 250 square feet) on flat ground are probably best designed with a single level. However, a sloping lot might present an opportunity for a bilevel design. The upper main level would be the larger, more public area; the smaller, lower level would be more private. Steeply sloping lots will accommodate three or more levels.

By no means are you required to follow the terrain, especially if a single-level deck sticks out over a slope that provides you with a great view. In the end, letting the deck ride high might make the most sense. To help you visualize the possibilities for your own site, start sketching rough ideas as thumbnail drawings. Later, your thumbnails will evolve into more detailed drawings.

Access

Direct access is the primary consideration with an attached deck. The easier the access is to and from the kitchen, dining room, family room, or bedroom, the more you'll enjoy your deck. Two or even three doors often provide access. For example, the kitchen might have a single outside door, and the family room might have French doors or a sliding patio door. Sometimes the deck loops around the side of a house to include another outside door. Although this adds complexity and cost, it creates more convenience.

Proper access from the deck to the yard becomes crucial for fully enjoying your deck. Locating and designing steps to the turf involve both the practical and the aesthetic considerations. Decks are for leisure, so a wide stairway can echo their relaxed, graceful theme. No matter how many steps you have, 3 feet is a good minimum width, and with fewer steps, they can be even wider. For example, if it's only four or five steps to the yard, consider a 4- or 5-foot width. If it's only two or three steps, an entire side can become a stairway, perhaps punctuated with built-in or freestanding planters.

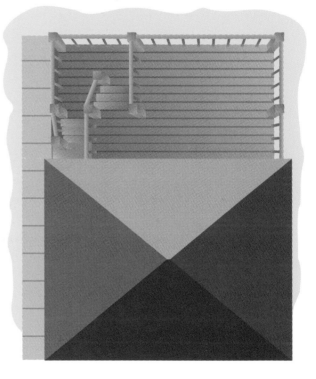

▲ *Access to the yard can be a key feature. Clockwise from bottom left: Simple stairways with brick landings ease the transition into the yard; some decks have stairs all the way around to give a wide-open appearance; if the deck is elevated, a stairway with landing adds architectural interest.*

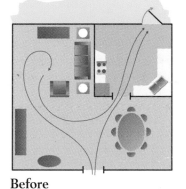

◄ *A double-wide door allows you to see more of the deck and extends the interior room outside, making both room and deck seem larger.*

PROBLEM **?** SOLUTION

Back-Door Plan

Sometimes a little remodeling is necessary to give you the access to the deck you need. It also may solve problems inside the house.

By adding a door and moving the existing kitchen door, as shown in the before and after illustrations, *right*, several problems are solved. The new door routes most traffic to and from the deck through the living room so that the work going on in the kitchen isn't interrupted. Rather than closing off the kitchen door to the deck, moving it retains the ability to take food directly from the kitchen out to the deck and at the same time frees up a corner of the kitchen for more cabinet and counter space or for a dining nook.

You also need to think about what kind of door you might add to maximize your view of the deck. You could expand a 32-inch half-window door to at least a 36-inch-wide full-window door (sometimes called a full-light door). If there's room, go for a double-wide door, sliding glass door, or a hinged door with a fixed all-glass sidelight. See pages 106 and 107 for instructions about how to install a door.

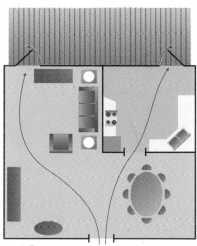

Before

After

> *A simple shade structure can extend the time you enjoy your deck into the hottest part of the day. Note the open sides of this structure, which allow cool breezes to flow across the deck.*

Environmental Factors

Sunlight and Shade

Sun and shade are important considerations in deck design. Too much or too little of either can reduce your ability to enjoy time on the deck. Ideally, you want a deck that delivers just enough of both.

If you discover the site gets too much sun, consider building a shade structure (discussed in greater detail on pages 76 and 77), which you can incorporate into your design or add after you finish the deck. A good long-term strategy includes planting some fast-growing shade trees.

But watch out for too much shade. Summer shade is important, but sunshine during spring and fall will extend your deck usage throughout the year.

DESIGN DETAIL

Sun Check

When you have a good idea where to locate your future deck, check out the site on a sunny day, preferably in spring or summer when the leaves are out.

On attached decks, south-facing decks get the most overhead sun. Shade will have to come from trees near the deck. Exposures to the east or west will get low-angle morning or afternoon sun. A solid fence, trellis, or low- to medium-height trees near the deck's perimeter will provide shade. A deck facing north gets some shade from the house, especially with remodeled wide-roof overhangs.

View

Most decks deliver the views seen from the house, so try to position a deck to take in the best and shield the rest. If you elevate your deck, use a steady stepladder to survey the view in different directions from the approximate deck height. If your site lacks a desirable view, you may want items that add visual interest on and around the deck, such as planters or screens that block eyesores. Enhance distant views with landscaping, unless lot lines are so close that only fencing will do. Some people put up fencing first to block an undesirable view while new plantings grow up and out.

Rain and Snow

Downpours will dampen any deck gathering, so protecting your guests with an extra-wide over-hang from the roof may save a party when the weather doesn't cooperate and produces rain instead of sunshine. If you live in a wet climate, a deck that's half covered and half open may serve you best.

Snow generally presents a concern where accumulations reach several inches. Building codes have built-in structural requirements that can handle snow loads, but if you live where heavy snowfall is common, consult building officials or an engineer to ensure deck strength.

Air Currents

You must also consider wind, especially strong wind. A gentle breeze refreshes on a summer evening, but hearty gales make the deck less comfortable. Choose a protected location or build well-braced wind screens to blunt the wind.

Experts' Insight

Plan for Privacy

For all its good design, a deck can fall into disuse because of a crucial oversight—a lack of privacy. No one is comfortable when they're completely on display. If building a deck attached to your house restricts you from putting it in a secluded area, there are some ways you can make up for a lack of privacy.

■ Bend part of the deck around to a more secluded side of the house

■ Build a deck-mounted privacy fence

■ Plant fast-growing shrubbery to screen out more distant houses as shown, *right*

■ Consider a secluded remote deck rather than an attached deck to deliver total privacy

Legal Considerations

Like most major home improvements, a deck addition must be done in compliance with local zoning laws and national and local building codes. To make sure everything goes just right from start to finish, you are required to submit plans to your town or county building department for its approval and to obtain a building permit. Depending on its policies, the building department also will inspect your project once, twice, or more to make sure it's going according to the approved plans.

Government supervision ensures that your design will be properly built—strong and safe. Remember, too, that building ordinances and codes prevent your neighbors from doing things that you might not like. So the bureaucracy you have to plow through to get your plans approved also might protect you from someone building an eyesore inches from your property line. Failing to comply with codes could result in the disaster of your having to remove what you've built. While this is rare, it's best to go through the approval process and avoid the hassle in the first place.

In any event, it's up to you, not your town, to initiate these official proceedings and find out what's required by zoning rules, possible added restrictions and other property conditions, and building codes.

What to do now: Obtain some printed information about local regulations that may affect your project. Find the information you need by calling your county building offices, telling them what you propose to do, and asking for any applicable material.

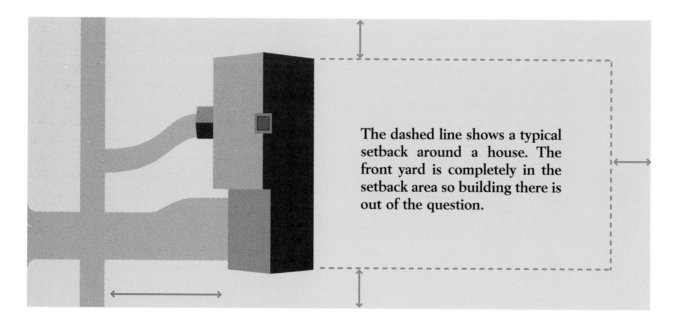

The dashed line shows a typical setback around a house. The front yard is completely in the setback area so building there is out of the question.

Zoning and Other Restrictions

One ubiquitous code concern is setback, which refers to the area next to a property line where new construction is restricted or forbidden. Side setback requirements tend to be more forgiving than those of front and rear setbacks. For example, a typical setback requirement might be 15 feet to the sides but 45 feet in front and back. Zoning and building codes adopted by your community determine setback, and you must investigate both before building a deck.

You may find that your house exceeds a current setback requirement. This usually means the house was built before the rules were established and was thus "grandfathered" or protected by its status as a pre-existing structure. Unfortunately this doesn't mean a new deck also can exceed the setback. The only way it can is for the project to be granted a variance to the existing zoning by your town's planning or zoning board.

Building a deck that doesn't comply with zoning and building codes can be risky. It literally can be condemned and may have to be razed, moved, or drastically changed. However, all is not lost if the only way you can build a deck is to get a zoning variance. Your chances of receiving a zoning variance increase greatly if you anticipate concerns of neighbors and those of the zoning board. It's usually helpful to have someone familiar with appearances before the zoning board help you prepare your request for a variance. If you don't know of anyone who's asked for a variance, ask your real estate agent; they usually know of, or can find the name of, someone who might be able to help you.

Check your property deed, too. It may include an easement that gives others permission to use part of your property for a specified purpose. For example, a previous owner may have granted an easement to bury a water line under your property. An easement would permit access for possible servicing. If so, you wouldn't want to build in the area specified because the water department may need to dig up the ground under your deck.

You also want to avoid construction over any underground utilities. If you have a septic system, make sure you know where the drain field is. Locate water lines, sewers, and buried gas, electric, or telephone lines. You can call your utility companies for these locations and ask them how deep the various lines are buried. Many times they will come and mark the location of the lines for you. They'd rather mark existing utilities than have to fix them when someone digs into them in order to place a deck footing.

What to do now: Look into setback requirements and see if your property deed contains restrictions and locate any buried utilities.

Building Codes

As already noted, these regulations can affect your plans. Often they specify minimum structural requirements for materials such as posts, beams, decking, and railing structures. (See Phase 2: "All About Materials." Most building codes also specify safety features such as the proper heights for deck and stair railings (usually 3 or 4 feet high). You may, however, have to build in additional safety features for toddlers who could crawl under railing guards or poke their heads between stairway uprights, called balusters.

Code regulations may very well do some of your designing for you. As with zoning requirements, building codes also enjoy the force of law, and your deck will be inspected to make sure it is being built according to the plan for which you were issued the building permit. If you're in doubt about any of these restrictions, ask questions, starting at your county building department, until you have answers.

What to do now: Chat with your county's building inspector to learn about specific code, design, and construction requirements.

A Word of Caution

Many do-it-yourselfers sidestep the zoning and code issues and just go ahead and build their deck. But they do so at their peril. If you ever wish to sell your house, it will be inspected before the deed can transfer hands, and often the owner will have to bring the house up to code for the sale to take place. Bringing a pre-existing deck up to code is difficult. It is far easier to build it to code in the first place and rest assured it's a properly built, legal structure that won't cause problems.

▲ *Railings can double as benches, expanding seating areas without taking up deck space.*

Deck Railings

Most building codes require railings for decks that rise 2 or more feet from the ground. Railings must be 36 to 42 inches high (check your county code for the exact requirement) with no more than 6 inches between horizontal rails or between balusters and other vertical members.

Railings primarily prevent falls, but this function doesn't preclude a creative design. The most common railings are similar to the traditional picket fence except that the balusters usually end below the cap rail. Typical framework consists of 4×4 posts spanned by horizontal 2×4 or 2×6 cap rails and 2×4 bottom rails, with the balusters providing style. To prevent sagging railings, keep the spans between posts at less than 6 feet. When putting up the first baluster, check it with a level to ensure it's plumb. To keep the balusters aligned, hold a spacer at the top and bottom while fastening each end in place. A completely enclosed rail, faced with siding and open only at the bottom for drainage, provides more privacy and also can block wind.

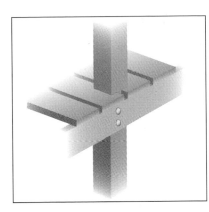
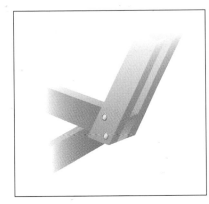
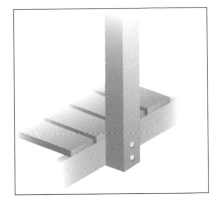

Attaching Railing

Some posts that support beams also can extend above the deck and support the railing or any built-in elements you may have added to your design, as shown *above left*. You also can bolt short posts to perimeter joists or beams at an angle, *above center*, providing a new design option and using them as backrests for benches as shown on the *facing page*. Always use two bolts when bolting a post to the structure below it, *above right*, so it cannot pivot at the connection point and topple over.

THE RIGHT STUFF

You don't need a lathe to make stylish additions for your railings. Ready-made parts are important alternatives. For example, home centers now feature many styles of decorative railing parts. Some of these are pictured *below left*, clockwise from top: two traditional-style balusters (also called spindles), a post cap, and the finial that goes on top of the cap. All can be found made of redwood, cedar, and pressure-treated lumber. The results can be spectacular as shown *below right*.

Budget

The best aspect about decks is that they are less expensive than most other home additions. In fact, as the cost tables on pages 55 through 57 show, when you build it yourself, a deck qualifies as bargain living space. Because decks are so popular, they also make homes more marketable and valuable. Buyers will see an addition they may pay an extra $5,000 for but that might have only cost you around $2,000 for the materials. The last thing you may want to think about is selling that beautiful deck you're about to build. But if it's any comfort, you can rest assured that your efforts and expenses will increase the value of your home substantially.

For basic designs using the least expensive lumber, you can expect to pay from about $6 to $8 per square foot of deck area. Even if you choose top-of-the-line redwood lumber or want a hot tub, material costs are still reasonable, anywhere from $20 to $35 per square foot. When you consider that hiring out the job will perhaps double or likely triple your costs, a do-it-yourself deck looks attractive. Keep in mind that any extra features, such as shade structures, built-in benches, or planters, require additional materials and add to the cost per square foot.

If you're not a do-it-yourselfer or you simply do not have the time to devote to building your own deck, concentrate on designing the deck you want then finding a builder who can work within your budget. Use the sample budgets on pages 55 through 57 to get a rough idea of how much a builder might charge.

Money $ Saver

What It All Costs

These sample budgets provide the costs for material and for a general contractor to do all the work. You can see your savings in doing the work yourself. In fact, the economy of a do-it-yourself deck might buy you a larger design or higher-quality materials. The contractor's fee assumes overhead costs and a reasonable profit for the builder. Remember that the various prices shown on pages 55 through 57 represent national averages and actual prices in your area may vary.

(This information was excerpted with permission from *Exterior Home Improvement Costs*, R.S. Means Company, Inc.; P. O. Box 800, Kingston, MA 02364–0800, 1994. The book contains cost information for 67 other projects and is a companion to *Interior Home Improvement Costs*.)

▲ *Innovative design can reduce your budget. This deck was designed with a removable section for faucet access. Without this feature, the homeowner would have incurred substantial cost in moving the faucet.*

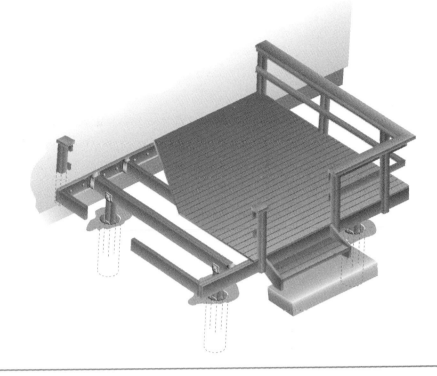

Key for table abbreviations
C.F.–Cubic Foot
C.Y.–Cubic Yard
d–Pennyweight of Nails
Ea.–Each
lb.–Pound
L.F.–Linear Foot
O.C.–On Center
S.F.–Square Foot

Ground-Level Deck

Description	Labor in Hours	Quantity	Cost of Materials
Layout, excavate post holes	0.5		
Concrete, filed mix, 1 C.F. per bag for posts		4 bags	$ 32.40
Forms, round fiber tube, 8" diameter	2.1	10 L.F.	21.00
Deck material, pressure-treated posts 4"×4"×4'	0.6	16 L.F.	34.75
Headers, 2"×6"×10'	1.3	40 L.F.	36.96
Joists, 2"×6"×8'	2.3	72 L.F.	66.33
Decking, 2"×4"×10'	8.2	280 L.F.	171.36
Stair material, pressure-treated stringers 2"×10"×3'	0.2	6 L.F.	11.02
Treads, 2"×3"×3'6", 3 per tread	0.4	12 L.F.	7.34
Landing, precast concrete, 14" wide	0.1	4 L.F.	17.04
Railing material, pressure-treated posts, 2"×4"×3'	0.9	30 L.F.	18.36
Railings, 2×4" stock	1.5	52 L.F.	31.82
Cap rail, 2×6" stock	0.8	26 L.F.	24.02
Joist and beam hangers, 18-gauge galvanized	0.3	7 Ea.	5.38
Nails, #10d galvanized		8 Lb.	7.20
Bolts, ½" lag bolts, 4" long square head with nut and washer	1.0	18 Ea.	18.79
Totals	20.2		$503.97
Project Size 8×10' Contractor's fee including materials			$1,490.85

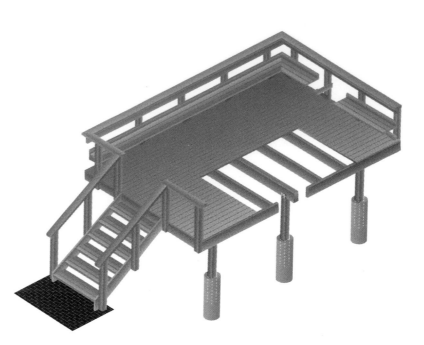

Key for table abbreviations
C.F.–Cubic Foot
C.Y.–Cubic Yard
d–Pennyweight of Nails
Ea.–Each
lb.–Pound
L.F.–Linear Foot
O.C.–On Center
S.F.–Square Foot

Elevated Deck

Description	Labor in Hours	Quantity	Cost of Materials
Layout, excavate post holes	0.5		
Concrete, filed mix, 1 C.F. per bag for posts		6 bags	$48.60
Forms, round fiber tube, 8" diameter	3.1	15 L.F.	31.50
Deck material, pressure-treated posts 4"×4"×7'	1.7	48 L.F.	104.26
Headers, 2"×6"×16'	2.3	64 L.F.	82.18
Joists, 2"×8"×10'	4.3	120 L.F.	154.08
Decking, 2"×4"×12'	16.8	576 L.F.	352.51
Stair material, pressure-treated stringers 2"×10"×10'	0.8	20 L.F.	36.72
Treads, 2"×3"×3'6", 3 per tread	2.0	70 L.F.	42.84
Landing, brick on sand, laid flat, no mortar 4.5 bricks per S.F.	2.3	16 S.F.	50.88
Railing material, pressure-treated posts, 4"×4"	1.7	48 L.F.	104.26
Railings, 2×4" stock	2.8	96 L.F.	58.75
Cap rail, 2×6" stock	1.5	48 L.F.	44.35
Bench material, seat braces, 2×4"	3.1	108 L.F.	66.10
Joist and beam hangers, 18-gauge galvanized	0.6	12 Ea.	7.63
Nails, #10d galvanized		15 Lb.	13.50
Bolts, ½" lag bolts, 4" long square head with nut and washer	1.6	28 Ea.	29.23
Totals	45.1		$1,227.39

Project Size	10×16'	Contractor's fee including materials	$3,477.79

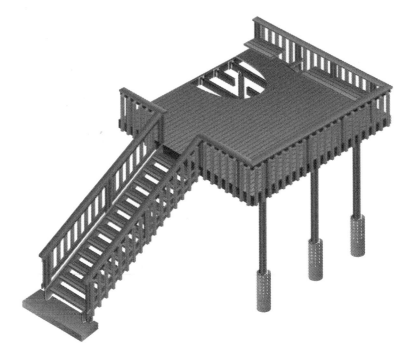

Elevated Redwood Deck

Description	Labor in Hours	Quantity	Cost of Materials
Layout, excavate post holes	0.5		
Concrete, filed mix, 1 C.F. per bag for posts		6 bags	$48.60
Forms, round fiber tube, 8" diameter	3.1	15 L.F.	31.50
Deck material, pressure-treated posts 4"×4"×4'	3.0	72 L.F.	460.80
Headers, 2"×6"×10'	0.7	48 L.F.	307.80
Joists, 2"×6"×8'	2.1	144 L.F.	921.60
Decking, 2"×4"×10'	9.0	504 L.F.	1,614.82
Stair material, pressure-treated stringers			
2"×10"×3'	3.9	32 L.F.	255.36
Treads, 2"×3"×3'6", 3 per tread	2.6	144 L.F.	461.38
Landing, precast concrete, 14" wide	0.1	9 S.F.	38.34
Railing material, pressure-treated posts, 2"×4"×3'	2.2	120 L.F.	384.48
Railings, 2×4" stock	1.3	72 L.F.	230.69
Balusters 1×6" stock	8.7	240 L.F.	192.96
Cap rail, 2×6" stock	2.0	96 L.F.	460.80
Bench material, seat braces, 2×4"	0.9	48 L.F.	153.79
Joist and beam hangers, 18-gauge galvanized	0.6	12 Ea.	9.22
Nails, #10d galvanized		14 Lb.	12.60
Bolts, ½" lag bolts, 4" long square head			
with nut and washer	1.0	18 Ea.	18.79
Totals	41.7		$5,603.53

Project Size	12×12'	Contractor's fee including materials	$9,438.27

Problem Sites and Solutions

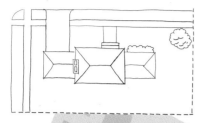

Many homeowners do not live on a lot ideally suited for deck construction. If your property presents you with one of these problems, don't let it deter you. Working within some constraints often can bring out creative solutions.

Shallow Lot

A lot that doesn't lend itself to an expansive deck doesn't necessarily keep you from building a deck. A long, narrow deck, say 8×30 feet, might just fit the bill. Note how the sample design wraps around the side of the house and includes a new stone walk for access to the front of the house. The design also uses a sliding door for access to the house. A hinged door would have required valuable deck space for the door to swing open.

Narrow Lot

Decks for narrow lots with close neighbors often are built no larger than the width of the house. In this example, the deck uses exactly the same width of the house. High screens attached to the deck will afford deck loungers privacy from the eyes of neighbors.

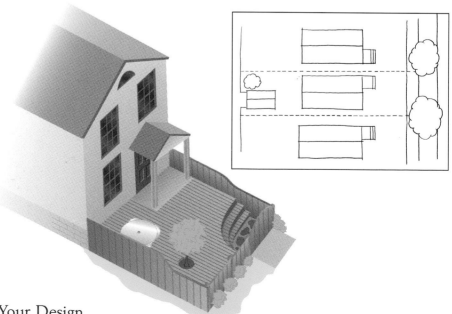

Unsightly View

By imagining views in advance and adjusting your design, you can avoid having to look at a bad view from your nice deck. Here the deck not only includes an attached privacy fence, but the deck also is angled so activity, seating, and the natural flow of traffic cause people to look away from an unsightly view.

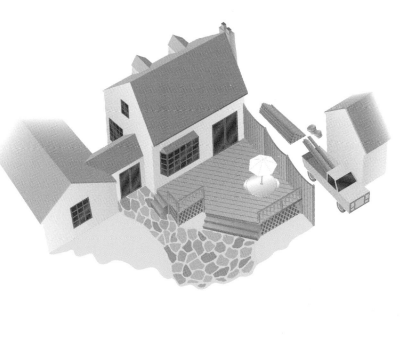

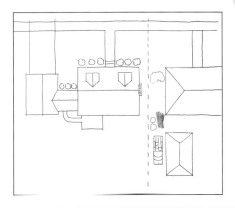

Steep Slope

Steep slopes are both an advantage and disadvantage. Because the ground drops quickly away from the house, a deck on a steep slope can give some of the best sweeping views. However, it also can be difficult to build. Whether the ground slopes down or up from the deck site, a multilevel deck that follows the contour of the site is almost always the best solution. Not only does it give complexity to the feel of the deck, but it also keeps the height of the outer edge of the deck down, and therefore reduces the difficulty of construction.

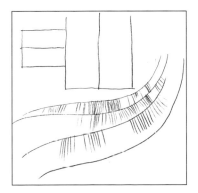

Within Limits

So far we've covered the wide range of general planning issues and options for decks. Now it's time to move on to getting your ideas down on paper. This stage of planning and design will take you beyond your thumbnail sketches all the way to plans on paper.

Know the Lot

You'll need to make an accurate, though not necessarily formal, survey of your lot. From that make a simple map. Do this by determining the lot's dimensions and boundaries. If your home sits in a development, the contractor or architect may have a detailed plan, or previous owners may have completed one. Another possible source is a loan plat, a map of the property that generally accompanies the land title and is filed at a local record office, the courthouse, or with the mortgage holder. It usually shows at least the lengths of the lot lines. The directions in which they run usually are described in the deed or title, which also will sometimes show location of the house and any other structures, and indicate the location of easements. In the unlikely event you cannot find a lot plan, you can make one of your own, again using the description of the property in the deed. Measure your lot with a flexible 50- or 100-foot tape—one that winds up on a reel—and watch for corner markers from previous surveys. If your lot is irregularly shaped, you can use a compass to site the angles from corner to corner. If all this proves too difficult or you want to be certain where your lot lines are, hire a professional surveyor.

It's a good idea to transfer your lot map onto graph paper so you can more easily sketch elements to scale. (Make a few copies of the basic lot plan so you can sketch different ideas.) Let each square on the graph paper equal a few feet on the ground at any scale that allows the whole lot to fit on one piece of paper. For example, if one square equals 5 feet, an 8½×11-inch sheet of ¼-inch graph paper will hold a lot as large as 220×180 feet, which is nearly an acre.

After you've established the lot lines, measure to determine the position of your house and transfer that measurement to the graph paper. Be as accurate as you can when determining both the house's distance from the lot lines and its shape, or "footprint." Also indicate door and window locations and walls of rooms that might be adjacent to the deck.

Locate and record the lot's other features on the plan. Do this by measuring out from the corners of your house and projecting lines by setting temporary stakes at 10-foot intervals. Mark their location on your map. Then measure from the stakes to your walkways, driveway, walls, fences, other structures, and any other element that isn't turf, such as trees, bushes, and flower beds. Record everything on your lot plan. A map such as this will help you visualize not only the way a deck relates to the house and whole property but also the changes you could make to the property to improve the deck.

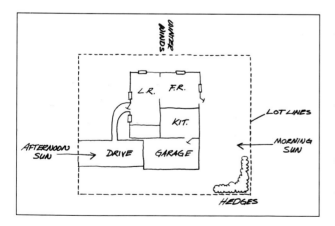

▲ Use graph paper, a sharp pencil, a steel measuring tape, and the legal description of your property to create an accurate overhead view of your lot.

DESIGN DETAIL

Improving Your Lot

The before lot plan, *below left*, shows a property with several common drawbacks. Immediately behind the house, the most likely spot for a deck, a neighbor's garage makes for a poor view to the left. A hedge blocks the one good view, straight out from the back of the house. Also, any deck placed on the back of the house would be exposed to wind in the cooler months and to direct sunlight in summer.

When you survey your own lot, consider which of these and other features you would change or preserve, according to their impact on your deck and in terms of your own preferences. You don't have to put off your deck building until the yard is right. Decide instead which improvements give the most benefit for the least money and do them soon. Plan others for over the next couple of years.

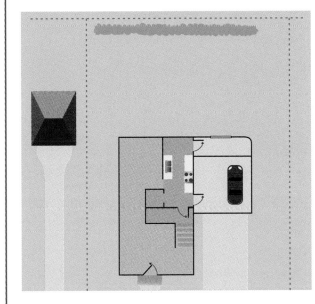
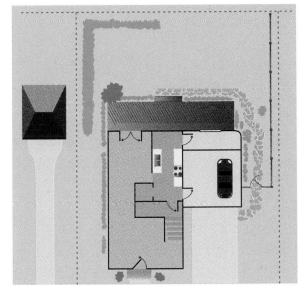

The after plan, *above right*, shows some possible improvements. Notice the structural and planting changes. Transplanting the hedge blunts both cooler winter winds and the view of the neighbor's garage to the left. A decorative gate and privacy screen on the right not only provide stylish access to the backyard, but also screen the neighbor's yard to the right.

Also, a fast-growing tree has been planted to give shade to the deck side most exposed to summer sunshine.

Structural changes have switched access to the backyard from the galley kitchen to the dining room, thereby improving traffic flow in the house and increasing space in the kitchen.

Deck Sketching

With your yard improvements well in hand, you can get to the main task: the deck plan. Use the tracing paper to make overlays of possible designs by lightly sketching in the outlines and basic details (stairs and so on) in the area of your first choice. (See "Anatomy of a Deck" in Phase 2, page 26, for a look at all the structural and finish elements.) Adjustments at this point involve simply laying down a fresh sheet or, as you get closer to a final plan, gently erasing lines and moving things around. To start, look at your first thumbnail sketches and draw ideas from them.

Keep making changes until you're well satisfied. Doing this at the planning stage, making changes on paper, is far less painful and expensive than after you've started digging and building.

Once you're satisfied with your lightly drawn project, use a plastic triangle and scale to draw heavier lines on the tracing paper. A compass will draw regular curves. Be sure to note the radius as you lay out a curved area. Later you can scale this radius up to its actual length by using a string and transfer it directly to the work site. For any irregularly curved areas, a French curve (with multiple curved shapes) will provide you with a template to draw smooth lines.

DESIGN DETAIL

Fitting Benches

The following illustration shows common sizes for benches, the most common built-in element of decks. Before you just follow the common sizes, find benches and chairs you find comfortable and measure them so you have a good idea of your desired bench size if it is any different than standard. Make sure your deck sketch has adequate space for freestanding furniture, too.

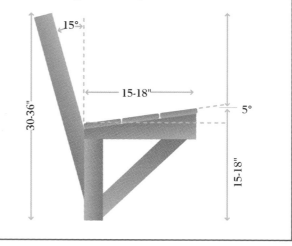

Experts' Insight

Questions You Must Ask

Go back to the overhead view of the lot and continue to question your design.
- Is the deck roomy enough?
- Is the size you're planning right for the furnishings you want?
- Does the deck stairway land on a clean walkway or gravel so people don't track dirt?
- Is it close enough to the kitchen and dining area to be convenient?
- Will it create any noticeable house-to-deck traffic problems?
- Will it ease or interfere with a swimming pool, garden, or other yard area?
- Is the project too close to a street, a neighbor's driveway, or your own driveway?

Grounding the Plan

Grounding the plan serves as a reality check. In this step you transfer the deck's dimensions from the tracing paper to the building site itself. Absolute accuracy isn't essential, but you want to get an idea of the size and look of the project.

Use a string line and 1×2 or 2×2 stakes to outline rough dimensions of the project as shown, *right*. For on-ground decks and those raised only a few feet, you can avoid driving stakes and running out string by using flour to outline the deck area. Lay out the square corners with a carpenter's framing square and measure the distances with a tape measure. Start from a corner near or touching the house, and use the framing square to keep things on line. This will give you sufficient accuracy for this preliminary check.

Stakes and strings are a must, however, for yards with anything more than a gentle slope and for decks that must be raised several feet. When you lay out a slope, position stakes in the ground at intervals and stretch a cord between them. This will give you an accurate measure of horizontal distance. Check with a line level to ensure the cord is always horizontal (see tip, *right*). Place the stakes high enough to raise the strings to the planned height of the deck. Stakes that are more than 5 or 6 feet tall may need bracing to keep them straight.

When you've completed the outline, walk around in it and get an idea of the space. It may seem as if you're adding a very large, spacious deck, but remember, when finally built, the railings, furniture, and built-in elements will detract from the open space of the deck.

As a last check of your design decisions, take snapshots of the house where the project will be after you've put up the stakes and string. Tape tracing paper over the photographs, and sketch in a three-dimensional view of the deck as best you can, with all elements you plan for the deck. This will give a better picture of the deck's fit.

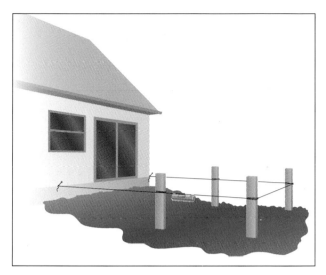

TOOLS TO USE

Level Help

To establish level lines over long distances, builders will use a transit—one of those scopes you see on tripods at construction sites. You can do the same with simpler, easier leveling tools.

■ Line Level—Hang a line level, *below*, from a taut string in the middle of its run between two points, and move one string end until the line-level bubble is centered.

■ Water Level—Use a long, clear tube or a length of garden hose with clear tubing at the ends. When filled with water, the water line at both ends is at the exact same level. That lets you fix one end to the known height and find its horizontal extension many feet away.

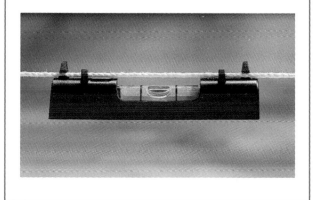

The Final Plan

Once you've made all your changes, the rough plan should be at or near its final form. Transfer the deck plan from the tracing paper to a copy of the original plot plan. This will help you make larger-scale drawings that will serve as the plans you submit for a building permit and as your working plans. To get a building permit, develop a lumber list, and have a useful construction guide, your final plans will have to include an overhead or plan view (the deck as seen from directly overhead) and elevations, views from all four sides or three sides of an attached deck. If you haven't drawn plans before, it's a good idea to request some guidance from local officials who grant building permits so you know you'll have exactly the elements they want.

You should draw the plan and elevations on a scale of ½ inch equals 1 foot. An 8½×11-inch piece of paper will contain a plan view as large as 16×21 feet, so for larger decks buy a tablet of sizable drawing paper, such as 11×17 inches, or you can buy paper on a roll.

To get a permit you'll need some construction details like depth of footings and lumber sizes labeled in the drawing, in addition to specific framing or fastening techniques. Other examples may include how you'll secure posts to the footings, or how you'll construct railings and built-in benches. You'll also need to provide a lumber specifications list so a building inspector can see that the deck will be structurally sound.

When you've completed your final drawings, make two sets of photocopies, keep the originals for yourself, and bring a copy to your building department to apply for your building permit. The department may request revisions. When you get approval, take your list to the lumberyard and start turning your plans into reality.

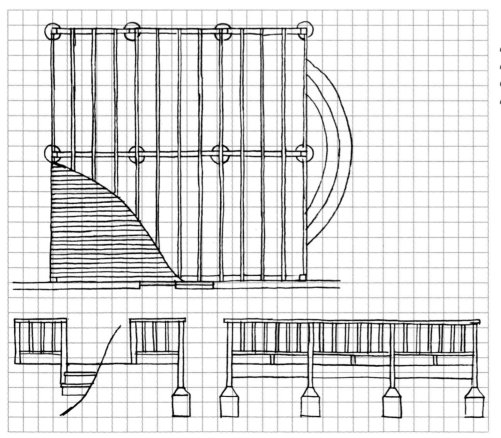

◀ *Plans you submit to a building department always include an overhead view as well as elevation views.*

What About Ready-Made Plans?

If you prefer building over planning, some sources offer ready-made plans. Many publishers, such as Better Homes and Gardens®, offer plans, *below*, that you can buy in home centers. Mail-order publishers of house plans, such as Homestyles in Minneapolis, offer designs that adapt to specific sites. Another source, the California Redwood Association, offers a Design-a-Deck kit that uses peel-and-stick templates for deck modules ranging from 4×8 feet to 14×20 feet. You can combine modules to make a larger deck and trim modules to a custom size. The kits also feature scale stick-on templates for stairs, furniture, planters, and outdoor grills.

Precut Deck Kits

If you want a simple deck—one that's neither large nor fitted with many custom features—you can use a precut kit. Some larger home centers and lumber retailers offer these complete packages for simple decks. Their best feature is usually the price. Their disadvantages are that they're difficult to find, you can only choose from one or two sizes, and they have only a limited number of styles to offer.

TOOLS TO USE

Designing with a Computer

Deck planning has entered the computer age in a couple of ways. Many building material and home center dealers offer a design service that allows you to view the deck three-dimensionally. You supply the key dimensions, and the computer, operated by a trained employee, does the rest. When you reach a final design, the computer generates a lumber and hardware list, complete with prices.

Other design programs function comparably with the home center software. Priced between $15 and $60, there are enough different versions to find one that runs on the type of computer you own.

Features include two- and three-dimensional views, and some programs let you "walk" over the deck's image on-screen and view it from several rooms inside the house. You can experiment with different sizes and shapes, stain colors, and furniture and built-ins. These programs automatically plug in lumber of the right dimension to satisfy any building code. You also can print the plan you want and bring it to your building department. Usually the programs also let you print out a complete lumber list that will help you get competitive bids for materials.

Special Features

After choosing a deck design, you might want to spice it up with features that add utility and comfort.

Although you've developed your basic deck design and have put most of it down on paper, give a thought to including some more features to make your deck exactly the one you've wanted. Think of your deck as an outdoor living room that's more than just a rectangle. Now add the items that make a deck more livable and more enjoyable. Your options include:

■ Landscaping
■ Planters
■ Benches and tables
■ Privacy screens
■ Shade structures
■ Doorways
■ Hot tubs and swimming pool surrounds
■ Outdoor kitchens
■ Lighting

This chapter covers all these special features in terms of design and what it might take to incorporate them. At this point you should have a sketch of the deck you're considering. Work these features into your basic design sketch to fine-tune how your deck will work and look.

➤ *Small features can make a big difference in the usefulness and look of a deck. Note the separate areas for different activities, the built-in planters and benches, and the trellis in back for climbing plants.*

Landscaping

▲ *If color is what you want, choose a flowering tree to shade one end of your deck. Consider all seasons when choosing plants—what may look great in spring may not be right come August.*

Like houses, decks need landscaping to soften that hard line between structure and ground. Decks can stand out more than houses, naked posts and all, so place greenery around the perimeter of the deck and even on the deck itself.

Landscaping and deck design should happen simultaneously; each can affect the other in terms of locating walkway routes, drainage, plant irrigation, and the size and placement of any on-deck planters and trellises.

As with house foundations, deck landscaping covers structural elements and eases the transition from deck to ground. With a mix of trees, shrubs, ground covers, and perennial and annual flowers, you can develop a continuous-perimeter bed following classic patterns or curving plants in and out from the deck line.

You may wish to use trees sparingly and place them away from the deck to account for their mature height and crown size; don't plant trees where they will grow and block your view. Place taller shrubs closest to the deck to provide a backdrop for shorter plantings. Shrubs should also be massed in groups and not mixed in among other single species. This also holds for flowers, except where restricted space prevents massing.

Save yourself a lot of time for enjoying your deck by choosing low-maintenance plants, such as disease-resistant shrubs that don't need frequent pruning. Plants indigenous to the area you live in are always a good choice because they usually can handle the weather you receive. Ground covers cut down on weeding, and perennials reduce spring flower planting. A few annuals will add unique accents to most landscaping.

◀ *If you want raised beds in your yard, building a deck provides you with the opportunity of incorporating landscaping timbers into your design.*

▲ Landscape edging, decorative bark mulch, and rocks underneath the deck add visual appeal where it is often difficult to grow plants.

► Landscaping may be as simple as adding planters to your deck design for a splash of color from annuals.

Planters

▲ *Planters can be as simple as a four-sided box with feet. These boxes use miter-cut 2×10s for the sides and 2×2s for the feet.*

It's often worth adding nature to your deck design because it will tie the deck in with the outdoors. Planters overflowing with annuals and perennials can soften the hard lines of any deck. You can place built-in or freestanding planters nearly anywhere; planters also can run down a stairway providing a cascading flower effect. For a unique feature, you also can build a planter directly into the deck in a hazard-free spot.

You should use decay-resistant lumber for planters, 1½ inches thick, and fasten them with rust-resistant nails, screws, or bolts. Hot-dipped galvanized or stainless-steel connectors stand up well to the elements.

Two important plant-growing notes are: Make the planter 18 to 24 inches deep if you're planning to plant shrubs or bushes so there's enough soil; provide at least one drainage hole at the bottom, just like a flowerpot, so the plant doesn't suffer from wet "feet." Planters for annuals can be much smaller.

Line the planter with a waterproof material for longer planter life. Drainage holes shouldn't be directly over a joist, beam, or post because they may keep an area moist, leading to rot. If you build your own planters, raise them 3 to 4 inches above the decking to allow the boards to dry beneath the planters after it rains or snows.

▲ *For larger plants, planters can be attached to the side of a slightly raised deck to give the plants' roots plenty of room to grow.*

▲ *Here shallow planters are used as cap railings, and the builder put a beam above the rail for hanging pots. The geraniums provide a green visual wall on one side of the deck.*

➤ *A simple way to build a planter from remnants is to nail your decking material to four 4×4s. Alternate how the decking overlaps the 4×4s to give the planter visual appeal. Finish with a miter-cut top. Put this box over a regular pot with your plants inside. You may wish to move this planter every week or so, so the deck below doesn't stay wet.*

PHASE 3: Special Features 71

Benches and Tables

To make your deck more livable and welcoming, consider some built-in benches. They can help compose a perimeter railing and also serve to define and even divide the deck into areas.

Benches range from 15 to 18 inches high with seats at least 15 inches deep. You might prefer some deeper seats, up to 30 inches, for comfortable lounging. Benches within railings should have backrests unless they're on a ground-level deck; otherwise they can form simple platforms.

Benches connected to railings typically use the railing posts to support the back of the seats. The front edge can be supported by simple legs that are toenailed into the decking. Or, for a cleaner look that eliminates front legs, braces can run diagonally underneath the seating down to the railing posts. Use bolts to hold the benches in place so they can hold up under the strain of repeated use.

When bolting down benches, or any built-in structure, it's always a good idea to bolt the posts directly to beams or joists under the decking. You may need to cut notches in the decking for the posts to go through.

For your built-in eating area, plan for a table 28 to 30 inches high and 30 to 36 inches wide (see illustration, *facing page*). Fit the length of the table to your liking, with at least 24 inches for each place setting.

▲ *Built-in benches not only can serve as a place to rest but also as a barrier and design element.*

▲ *To make railings behind built-in benches more comfortable, slant them slightly so loungers may lean back comfortably.*

Saving Time

If you don't need a custom-built table or chair, or one that's bolted down, you can often buy prebuilt tables that match the style of most decks, like these prebuilt Adirondack chairs for a remote, platform deck.

➤ *If you know part of your deck will serve as an eating area, consider adding a built-in table made from the same materials as the deck so the table blends in.*

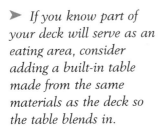

30-36"

28-30"

➤ *The greatest advantage of stand-alone benches is they can be moved to accommodate different seating needs, such as when you're entertaining guests.*

Privacy Screens

Like railings, privacy screens add style and function to a deck. Besides solving a privacy problem, they provide good shade and a base for climbing plants. Screens also help block or reduce excessive wind.

You may also need a screen that protects against insects. Fortunately, insect screens are simple structures that you can remove when the bug season ends. A stylish lattice panel can carry insect mesh on the inside to thwart both winged pests and prying eyes. Although a living trellis or hedge screen won't keep the bugs at bay, it can provide a lush backdrop and an extra measure of cooling (see page 76).

Deck perimeter supports also can function as the same posts for a privacy screen. You can bolt these posts to the deck surface or, better yet, to underlying joists or beams.

Don't limit your size considerations when designing a screen, although it makes sense to retain a compatible scale with other deck elements. If you wish to entirely block the neighbors' view from a second-story window, you might have to build an extremely high screen of about 10 to 12 feet. If this doesn't fit your house style or budget, you might have to live with a shorter screen that allows some visibility or move the deck to another location.

◄ *This louvered redwood screen is a little more complex to build than most screens, but it will protect privacy while allowing a gentle, cooling breeze to flow through.*

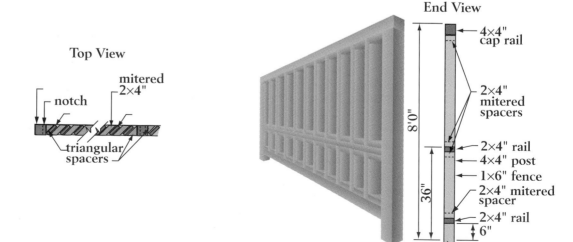

Top View

notch

mitered 2×4"

triangular spacers

End View

4×4" cap rail

2×4" mitered spacers

2×4" rail

4×4" post

1×6" fence

2×4" mitered spacer

2×4" rail

8'0"

36"

6"

▲ *A simple basket-weave fence is one of the easier visual screens to build. This redwood screen also provides a beautiful property line marker.*

End View

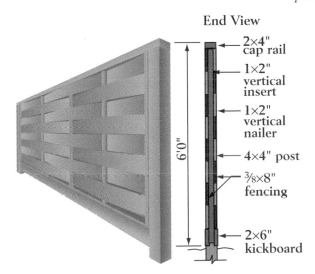

6'0"

2×4" cap rail

1×2" vertical insert

1×2" vertical nailer

4×4" post

³⁄₈×8" fencing

2×6" kickboard

Top View

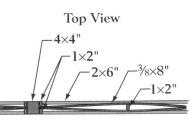

4×4"

1×2"

2×6"

³⁄₈×8"

1×2"

PHASE 3: Special Features 75

Shade Structures

Stylish shade structures can provide function and beauty for your deck. In addition to blocking sun, strategically placed boards in the form of slats, louvers, and lattice panels comprise attractive architectural features. The shading effect also can be increased by having the structure double as an arbor for a leafy climbing vine. You can arrange these structures to all but eliminate direct sunlight while still allowing plenty of daylight and ventilation. A slat or louver design allows you to vary the amount of sunlight by making some pieces removable.

Relatively small but well-fastened 4×4 posts can support these lightweight structures. To increase the shade in the mornings and afternoons, add vertical panels of lattice, made from woven bamboo or reed, or build in adjustable rolls of translucent, sun-resistant fabric or nylon shade cloth.

Lattice is a popular screen material. Commonly sold in 4×8-foot and 2×8-foot sheets, it's versatile, easy to install, and decorative. Standard panels are ½ inch thick, though some manufacturers also produce a heavier-duty panel made with thicker lath. About all you need to add to a lattice panel is framing. Lumberyards and home centers carry molding for this purpose.

▼ *Shade structures can block out most of the hot, midday sun, especially when you use climbing plants to give more shade. One advantage of using plants for some of your shade is that in cooler months the plant leaves fall off, letting the warming sun shine through.*

▲ *Premade lattice work can be used to provide the shade once the framework of your structure is up.*

▲ *Some structures are really designed more for visual appeal rather than the shade they provide.*

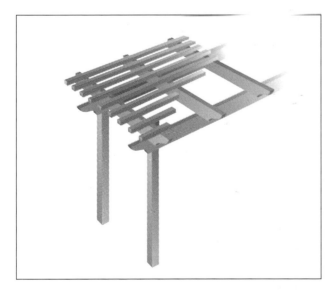

▲ *Shade structures often use three levels of wood with widely spaced larger lumber in the first two levels supporting closely spaced narrow strips on top. Three levels also provide adequate shade and the stability to support the wood, even in strong winds and storms.*

▲ *If your goal is visual and you wish to keep the area bathed in sunlight, widely spaced lumber can give you the effect of having a structure and block only a limited amount of light.*

Doorways

A wide glass door, one that provides an ample view, acts as the ideal deck entrance. French-style doors can provide a 48- to 72-inch opening when both doors are open. You also can buy a prehung door system that ranges from about 48 to 96 inches wide. Your framing for the door goes in place first (see how to install a door on pages 106 and 107), then you install the jamb and threshold, and rehang the door.

The doorway to your outdoor living area will affect your home's use and character. Before you settle on a location and size, consider all the factors—privacy, light, ventilation, and basic traffic patterns. Don't forget that big expanses of glass lose heat rapidly at night and gain it rapidly on sunny days. Minimize energy losses by choosing doors or windows with insulating glass and window treatments. Choose a style that fits the rest of your house.

◀ *Sliding doors no longer need to be just a vast expanse of glass. False muntins in the sliding door give it the style needed to fit with the rest of the house's design and prevent people or birds from running into the glass doors.*

◀ *A more contemporary look can be produced using doors like this one with large sidelights that allow more light to enter the room. Shop around before you select a style.*

◄ *Not only do larger doors allow more light, but they also give inside rooms a much bigger feel by showing the living space outside the door.*

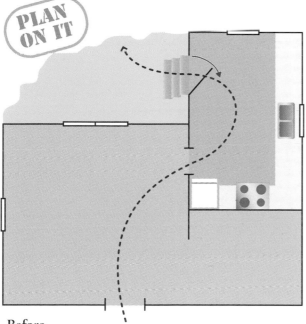

Before

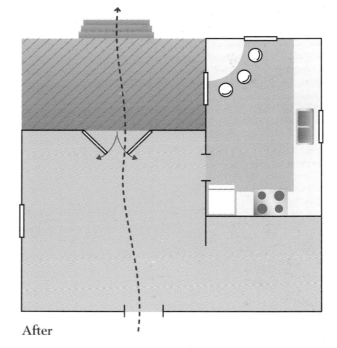

After

One of the great advantages of adding a doorway is that it gives you the opportunity to reroute traffic patterns in your house. Here the traffic has been shifted from interrupting work in the kitchen to going directly out the family room. In the process, the family room feels bigger because of the view of the living space outside the large doors. Also the closed-off kitchen corner now contains an eating area.

Hot Tubs

▲ *Raising the section of deck around the hot tub allows you to build the tub flush with the surface of the deck.*

Installing a hot tub requires a little imagination and a lot of planning, but you'll enjoy it for years. As an important, long-term investment, make sure you'll actually use a hot tub for the foreseeable future before you spend the time and money to install it.

If you decide to install one, determine where to place it based on existing landscaping and water and electrical service. Also decide if you want a sunny or shady location, if the view is important, or if you'll need a more private spot.

A standard family-size hot tub is 6 feet in diameter (about 30 square feet); a rectangular spa-style tub for four occupies about 49 square feet. To that area, add space for sitting and foot traffic. Plan for at least 100 total square feet with nearby sitting space and up to 140 square feet with sitting space that's right around the tub.

Most tubs hold 400 to 500 gallons of water, so they can weigh more than 2 tons when filled. This impacts the structural design of the deck. Unless the deck sits many feet off the ground, support the tub independently on a simple foundation of a poured concrete footing and concrete block walls (screened from view below the deck). Support for a raised tub requires heavy timbers and should be designed by an engineer or an experienced, licensed installer. You must also decide whether the tub will sit flush with the deck or a step below or above it.

Many local building codes require a fence or wall around a tub, so check with your local office to be sure. You must also plan space for a water heater, filter system, and other equipment that goes underneath a raised deck or is accessible through a panel.

▲ *Fences aren't the only way to make hot tubs more private; plantings will give your hot-tub area a sheltered, intimate atmosphere.*

▲ *In order to support the weight of all the water, use larger posts and joists under the hot tub, and place the joists closer together.*

Home Safety

Baby on Deck

The very ingredients that make decks useful, fun, and good-looking—stairways, railings, multiple levels, hot tubs, high elevations—also create safety hazards for children. Infants and toddlers should never be left alone on a deck, because they can get out of sight and into trouble faster than you might think. Minimize the dangers with a few simple precautions.

Doorways. Keep entry doors shut to prevent unsupervised exits. In warm weather, when doors are more likely to be open, screen doors always should be latched.

Railings. Put a temporary barrier between posts and balusters. If you're building a deck, space the balusters 4 inches apart or less.

Benches. The railings behind any built-in benches should be high enough, at least 24 inches above the seat, to prevent accidental tipping over. Round over any sharp edges on the benches for comfort and so children won't hurt themselves badly if they run into them.

Stairs. At the top of the stairs, put in a portable gate that can be latched. For wide

▲ *Like it or not, decks are a potential hazard to young children. Make them safe just as you would the inside of your home and increase your vigilance.*

stairs, narrow the opening with planters or other barriers, and block the remaining passage with a gate.

Hot tubs. Ideally, these should be fenced off, just like a swimming pool, with access only by way of a childproof gate. If that's not practical, use a secured hot-tub cover.

Swimming Pool Surrounds

If you have an in-ground swimming pool in your backyard or are planning to add one, consider a deck surround as an elegant alternative to flagstones or other masonry materials. For your above-ground pool, a raised surround can improve looks and livability.

If the reason you're building a deck is because you're adding a swimming pool at the same time, you may wish to consider installing an above-ground pool, especially if the deck you're planning has to be raised a few feet anyway. A raised deck could easily wrap around and be flush with an above-ground pool, giving it more of an in-ground appearance.

As the illustration on the *facing page* shows, a surround for an above-ground pool consists of standard, raised-deck construction. You can opt for a deck that fully or partially surrounds the pool. But don't feel obliged to have decking all the way around an above-ground pool; just make it fit your style, needs, and budget.

Decking for an in-ground pool normally covers the entire perimeter, but you can combine an on-ground main deck with a masonry surround, as your taste dictates. An in-ground pool usually has special requirements for drainage, as does a foundation for a house. If you build a surround that runs up to the edge of a pool, you need to have supports or footing set back away from the pool edge so they do not interfere with drainage and with the pool's plumbing, which typically is found buried around the edge of the pool.

▲ *Even when deck surrounds are simple they add comfortable living space that you might not otherwise have. This easily constructed surround is merely a thin, single-level deck built next to the pool.*

▲ *Build up the edge next to the pool with a custom fit by extending joists to the edge of the pool then cutting off the decking following the edge of the pool.*

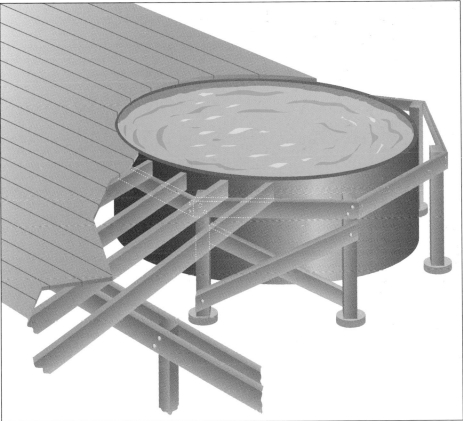

▲ Decks with siding can be used to add space around the pool and beautify the outside of an above-ground pool.

➤ By positioning posts around an above-ground pool, you can extend the decking right up to the edge, making it simpler to get in and out of the pool.

▲ *A single run of counter with cooker and sink can provide all the outdoor kitchen you need.*

Outdoor Kitchens

▲ *This cooking area was built from materials closely matching the materials used for the house.*

If you love the taste of outdoor cooking, why not incorporate an outdoor kitchen into your deck design? Not only will you get the savory taste you want, but you won't heat up the kitchen during the summer months of barbecue season.

Most people will just need space for a portable grill and a small preparation table, but you can have nearly a whole kitchen, complete with standard indoor amenities, in addition to a built-in or freestanding charcoal or gas grill.

An outdoor kitchen may well require a professional designer to think of everything that might be needed. For example, shade over the cooking area sounds appealing to keep things cooler in hot weather. But you'll have to be sure all outdoor cabinetry is weatherproof, which calls for rot-resistant wood and counters made of tile or stone. Completely drainable plumbing lines must prevent damage from freezing, and any power outlets must have ground-fault circuit interrupters (GFCI).

➤ *This small deck extension can accommodate outdoor cooking. It also allows traffic flow around the grill to remain normal when it's not in use.*

DESIGN DETAIL

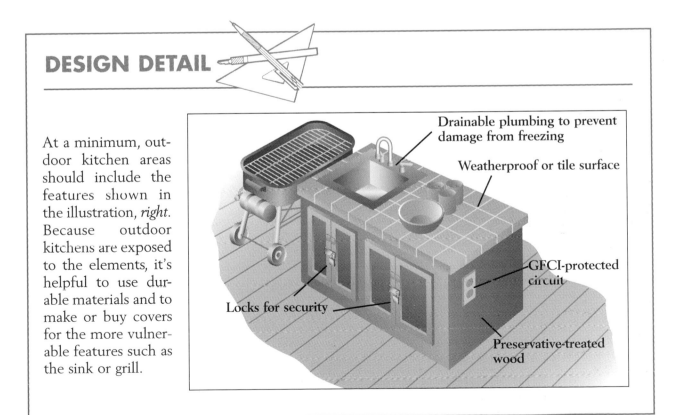

At a minimum, outdoor kitchen areas should include the features shown in the illustration, *right*. Because outdoor kitchens are exposed to the elements, it's helpful to use durable materials and to make or buy covers for the more vulnerable features such as the sink or grill.

Drainable plumbing to prevent damage from freezing

Weatherproof or tile surface

GFCI-protected circuit

Locks for security

Preservative-treated wood

Lighting

▲ *Less visible in the daytime, lights are placed to light the stairs at night and reduce the risk of stumbling.*

Nightfall need not be a signal to pack up and go inside. Outdoor lights will make your deck as inviting at night as during the day. Well-planned lighting not only gives you more deck time, but it also improves security and safety.

You can install outdoor light fixtures on and around the deck. Landscape lights can create dramatic accents with up lighting or down lighting and give the deck special night views. Fixtures mounted on the ground can direct light up through trees·and shrubs or along a fence.

Because of the popularity of decks for nocturnal use, lighting companies have designed products especially for them. For example, compact deck lights you can buy in any home center are designed to illuminate small areas, such as under the railings or steps.

Low-Voltage Lighting

Low-voltage wiring and fixtures present a convenient alternative for do-it-yourselfers, using a special transformer that "steps-down" standard 120-volt AC (alternating current) power to 12-volt direct current (DC). The current is so low the hazards of fire and shock are almost eliminated. Low-voltage lighting systems are convenient for many reasons; most plug into an outdoor outlet and allow you simply to plug in the transformer and carry on with lightweight cable you can bury just a few inches below the ground or staple under the deck and out of sight.

As you light your deck, place lights for decorative or functional effects, to highlight particular sections, or to illuminate stairways for safe night stepping. Outdoor lighting kits usually come with thorough installation instructions.

Outdoor Wiring

If you're adding electricity for wiring, consider adding more for such features as an outdoor music system, a rotisserie, and the blender that mixes your favorite drinks. With an attached deck, you might need only one or two outlets mounted on the house wall, in which case you face a fairly simple extension of an existing circuit. Before beginning a wiring project, check the specific requirements of your local electrical code. Local restrictions also may require a licensed electrician to do the work.

If you want to get power to a remote deck, you may need to add a new circuit to your service panel, then run it out of the house and bury it to reach your deck. Running wires underground involves digging trenches, so you may want to rent a trencher. Begin by planning your routes, including where you want to penetrate the house wall. As the illustration, *right*, shows, you'll need various specialized fittings for making conduit connections and turns.

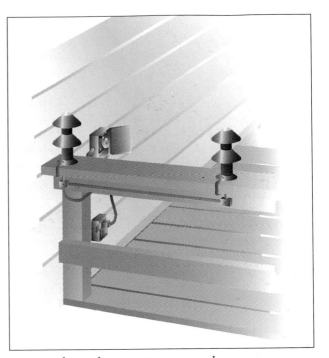

▲ *Most low-voltage wiring systems have a transformer with a timer in a small box you attach to the side of the house. From the box, a short cord extends to an outdoor receptacle for power, and the wire provided with the kit runs to the light.*

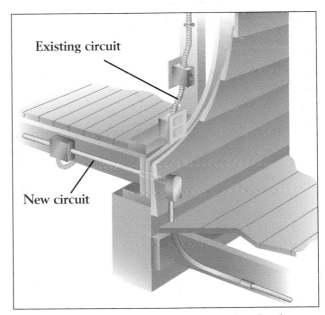

Existing circuit

New circuit

▲ *Electricity can be routed to your deck either by tapping into an existing circuit and creating a plug on the exterior wall, or by running a new circuit from the service panel and out the side of the house using specialized fittings and conduit.*

The Building Process

PHASE 4: It's time to turn those carefully made plans into a deck you can enjoy.

No more planning or designing, no more decks on paper or visits to the permit office—finally, it's time to build your deck.

Construction of a deck requires precision equal to all your planning work, so go slowly. Use the right tools and work safely (preferably with help). As always, measure twice to cut once. A few more weekends to make it right will reap years more of enjoyment.

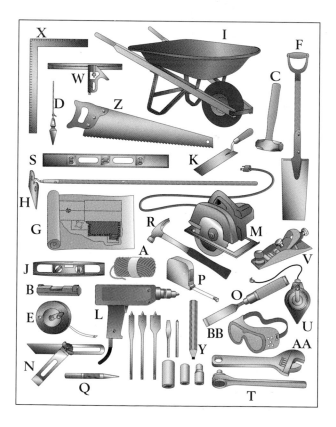

Tools

Use proper tools for an easier and better-built deck. Your project may require special tools, but the following list will work for most deck projects. (Note: You'll need tools for other phases, not simply those for which they're listed here.)

Site layout

- **A** Mason's line
- **B** Line level
- **C** Hand sledge
- **D** Plumb bob
- **E** 50-foot reel-type tape measure

◄ *Building a deck requires precision and patience. Spend a little extra time placing your posts exactly where they should be. A post that's even slightly askew will throw off your design at all subsequent stages.*

Post foundations

- **F** Spade shovel
- **G** Plan
- **H** Hoe
- **I** Wheelbarrow
- **J** Torpedo level
- **K** Concrete spatula
- ■ Post-hole digger or auger (optional)

Carpentry

- **L** ½-inch electric drill with wood-boring and screwdriver bits
- **M** Circular saw
- **N** Bevel gauge

- **O** 1-inch wood chisel
- **P** 25-foot tape measure
- **Q** Nail set
- **R** Framing hammer (straight claw)
- **S** 24-inch level
- **T** Socket or box wrenches
- **U** Chalk line
- **V** Block plane
- **W** Combination square
- **X** Framing square
- **Y** Carpenter's pencils
- **Z** Handsaw
- **AA** Adjustable wrench
- **BB** Goggles

Safety

Work Wear

Many do-it-yourselfers acknowledge the need for protective gear, but then, dangerously, habitually work without it. Flying wood, metal, and masonry chips will cause serious injury.

Manual labor makes a mess of your hands, so cover them. (However, don't use gloves when using power tools such as a circular saw. You'll be able to "feel" the tool better, and you won't get a glove caught and pulled into the blade or motor.) Button long-sleeve cuffs so they don't get caught and pulled into machinery.

Protect your eyes and consider ear protection such as headsets or plugs. Cutting wood with a circular saw demands wearing a simple dust mask. You also should wear sturdy work boots, preferably with steel-reinforced toes.

Safe Work Habits

In addition to wearing protective gear, you can minimize the potential hazards of deck building in the following ways.

■ Set up a spacious work area and keep it free of construction waste. Dispose of sawdust and lumber scraps in an approved landfill, bury them, or use them for kindling (pressure-treated lumber should not be burned, indoors or out).

■ When sawing pressure-treated lumber, always wash skin that has touched the material; wash exposed work clothes separately.

■ Stop working when you feel tired; take a break or quit for the day. Tired workers are the ones who make mistakes.

■ Never work when under the influence of alcohol or drugs, even cold medicines.

■ Lift properly, bending at the knees and using your legs rather than your back.

■ Use the proper tool for the job, read the operator's manual, and use the tool correctly.

■ Maintain all your tools well; keep cutting tools sharp, and store them safely.

■ Climb no higher than the third step from the top of a ladder.

■ Don't lean out from any ladder. Restrict ladder movements to one arm's length.

■ Store leftover flammable liquids, such as some finishes, in approved containers. Never store them in glass bottles.

■ Keep oily rags and similar wastes in a tightly sealed metal container, and dispose of them properly. Rags left in a pile may spontaneously combust. Your garbage collection service should have information on how to properly dispose of both oily rags and liquids such as stains and paints.

Deck Layout

Start with String

With your plan on paper, take a tape measure, mason's line, and several 1×2 stakes, and begin staking out the site. Build batter boards at each of the proposed deck corners as shown in the illustration, *right*, with 1×2 stakes and rails. Using this method will ensure you have square corners and exact post locations.

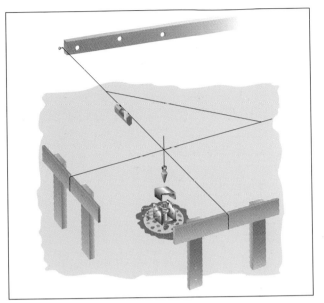

■ For an attached deck, lay out the height and length of the ledger on the siding; use string and a line level to make sure it's horizontal. For a freestanding, remote deck, establish the finished height relative to the ground, a distance based on the number of ground-to-deck steps in your plan.

■ Attach strings to the house at the bottom corners of both ends of the ledger and run them out to the batter boards; use the line level and keep adjusting the height of the batter board until the strings are horizontal.

■ Continue setting up batter boards and strings to locate all the post rows and individual post locations that your plan requires. The point at which two strings cross represents the corner, not the center, of a post.

■ For now, mark the general locations of the crossing points on the ground so you can dig the post footings. After digging, remove all strings so they are out of the way. When pouring concrete, put back the strings so you can determine the precise locations of piers or metal connectors.

MEASUREMENTS

Using the 3-4-5 Method for Perfectly Square Corners

When laying out your deck with string and batter boards, you must make sure that your right angles are truly right. Here's how.

■ Use a felt-tip pen to mark the strings 3 feet from the ledger corner and 4 feet from the corner along the house.

■ When the diagonal connecting these two points measures 5 feet, you have a right triangle; the corner angle will be 90 degrees.

■ If the distance from the 3-foot mark to the 4-foot mark doesn't equal 5 feet, then move the string attached to the batter board to obtain the 5-foot measurement. Any multiple of 3, 4, and 5 (6, 8, and 10 or higher) will also work. To double-check the squareness of your layout, measure the distances between opposite corners. If they are equal and the opposite sides of the deck are equal lengths, then you have a square layout; if not, move the strings until they are.

Site Preparation

For a low-level deck installation, you generally don't have to grade the site. Contours and grades of your deck site give it eye appeal and break the monotony of straight lines.

Carefully consider drainage to ensure the area remains dry and firm enough to support the structure. Dampness will cause wood rot, so keep in mind that grading should keep any moisture away from the wood of the deck. On a steep hillside, channel the surface runoff to minimize erosion. Building on a steep grade may involve special engineering to solve complex construction problems or satisfy municipal environmental requirements. For either case, you'll need to consult an expert.

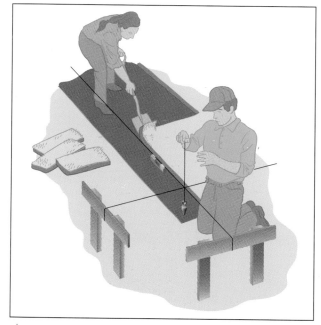

▲ *If you can, reuse sod from below the deck.*

Unless your deck will be a full story tall, the area underneath will be shaded and therefore unsuitable for most ground covers. However, deck builders must face the irony that even though grass won't grow beneath the deck, weeds will. So after you've taken up and reused the sod and erected the posts, you'll need to put down something to control weed growth.

Growth-control landscape fabric will prevent unwanted vegetation from growing and still allow drainage. You also can rake the ground clear and cover it with a sheet of 4-mil-thick black polyethylene plastic. Punch holes in the plastic every 6 feet with a nail to aid drainage. A layer of gravel, bark chips, or rock over the fabric or plastic provides a decorative finish and also anchors the sheeting in place.

Experts' Insight

Digging Post Footings

Before you begin, check with your county building department for specific requirements for type, depth, and strength of deck posts and footings, based on climate and terrain. You need to have footings that won't settle in soft soil, won't crack because of frost, and will provide a base that keeps the wood supports elevated above decay-causing moisture.

The holes for post footings should reach below the frost line in your area to prevent movement caused by freezing and thawing soil. This depth varies all over the country, so ask a builder, a concrete supplier, or your county building department for help.

A post hole is normally between 24 and 36 inches deep, depending upon the soil, the height of the post, and the depth of the frost line. If the soil at the base of the hole seems loose, compact it with a tamper. To reduce labor, rent or buy a post-hole digger. If your soil isn't too rocky and your design includes many post holes, a gas-powered auger is well worth the rental cost.

Framework

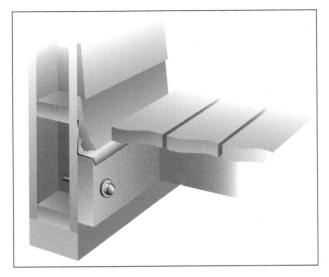

Attaching to Framed Wall

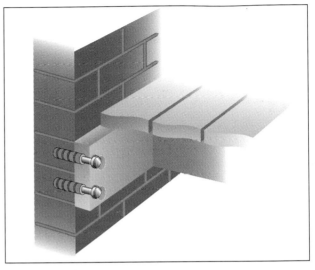

Attaching to Masonry

Attaching the Ledger Board

Depending on the design of an attached deck, the ledger board functions either as a beam upon which joists are set or as a rim or band joist from which the joists hang. In either case, fasten it tightly to the house.

On a framed wall, first remove any siding that would be covered by the ledger. If there is a layer of building paper or air-barrier material over the sheathing, leave it in place. Tuck a piece of Z-flashing up under the bottom edge of the siding so it lies over the top edge of the ledger, as shown *top left*. Bolt the ledger through the sheathing directly to the floor joists or to studs.

A masonry wall requires special fasteners spaced evenly along the board, as shown *top right*. Fasten the ledger directly to the wall, and caulk the seam between the ledger and wall to keep out moisture. If the wall is substantially uneven, use washers between the ledger and the wall to hold the ledger away from the side of the house and to even up the surface you're attaching the ledger to.

If you're attaching the ledger to a stucco wall, as shown *above right*, first cut a line with a circular saw into the stucco to fit the Z-flashing into.

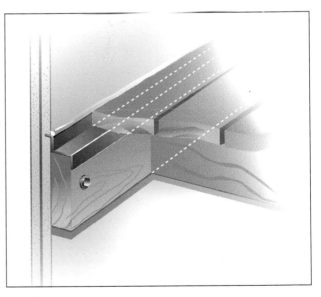

Attaching to Stucco

Use a blade in the circular saw that is designated to cut into stucco. Caulk the seam between the flashing and the stucco. Like masonry, stucco can be uneven. If it is, use washers between the wall and the ledger.

Securing the Posts

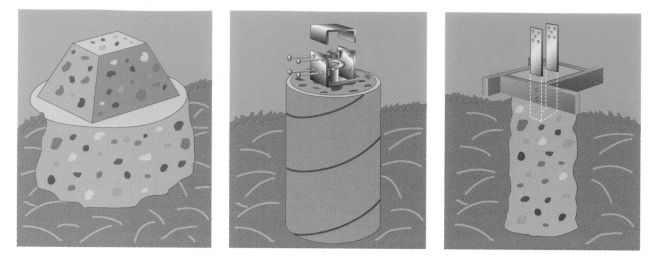

Before you do any concrete work, decide exactly how you will attach the posts to the footings, and make sure you have all the post bases you need. The illustrations, *above*, show a few options, all of which are designed to keep any moisture away from the post.

The method of attaching supporting posts to the footings or piers depends upon the kind of stress your structures must bear. You can set posts on precast piers above the footings you pour, *above left*. You might also embed a metal rod in the concrete, so it inserts into the post. This is an excellent method for decks not exposed to strong winds. With this method, place a barrier between the concrete and wood, such as a thin strip of sheet metal, roofing paper, or a coating of asphalt, tar, or other moisture barrier.

Some deck designs call for the post to be attached to the footing by some kind of metal fastener, *above center and above right*. Although these methods hold the wood just above the ground, it is still important to use lumber rated for ground contact. Some fasteners use a metal bolt imbedded in the concrete and a bracket which is attached to the bolt with a nut and to the post with screws, *above center*. A bracket imbedded in the concrete provides the most secure attachment and is ideal for most conditions, *above right*.

Mixing and Pouring Concrete

Mix the concrete in a wheelbarrow with a hoe and shovel. (If you have several post holes to fill, consider renting an electric mixer to speed the job.) Use water sparingly, as too much water will result in weaker concrete; err on the dry side.

If the footings will finish at or a little above ground level, make simple 2×4 forms to contain the topmost concrete and ensure a neat appearance. Set the forms to exactly level, and set the connectors to dead center on the footings. If the footings must rise several inches or a couple of feet, purchase ready-made forms made of cylindrical fiberboard. Available in different diameters, it can be cut with a saw to the length you need. When the holes and forms are ready, pour the concrete and poke a rod repeatedly into the footings to make the concrete settle.

Setting the Post Connectors

While the concrete is wet and workable, reset the layout strings and use a plumb bob to pinpoint the locations of the post connectors. (Again, string crossing points should denote a corner, and you must be certain which corner it is.)

Set the post connectors (metal rod or metal connector) square with the layout strings, level to the ground, and plumb. At this point, you can remove the layout strings to ease post placement. Allow at least 24 hours for the concrete to cure before stripping off the form. In dry climates, cover the tops of the footings with plastic to prevent dry, weak concrete.

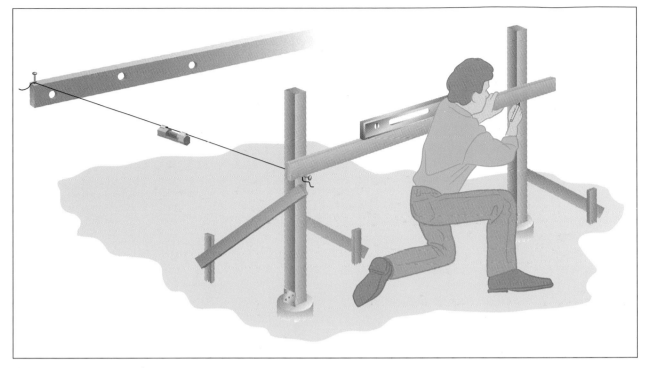

Cutting Posts to Height

Setting the Posts

Cut each post a little longer than its final height. When setting posts, use a carpenter's level to make them plumb. Check each post twice, making readings on sides at right angles to each other. Drive sturdy stakes near each post, and nail braces in place to keep posts plumb during construction, as shown *above*. Fasten the base of the posts with nails or bolts, depending on the connector.

To guard against rot, even when rot-resistant wood is used, coat the posts from their base up to about 24 inches with a preservative. Later, do the same on all wood joints and any other areas that might retain moisture.

Cutting the Posts to Height

When all the posts are in place, reattach the layout strings to the batter boards, and check them all with the line level to ensure they're level. With an attached deck, lines that come off the bottom edge of the ledger show where the top of the beam will be on each post. The actual cut line for the post is lower by the height of the beam. For example, with a 4×8 beam, the cut line is 7½ inches below the level at which the string passes the post. Draw the cut lines on all four sides with a square. If the joists will hang flush with the beam using metal hangers, the level lines show the bottom of the beam. Do not cut posts that double as a railing, screen, or bench support.

With a freestanding deck, determine the cut height for one post and make it the reference for all the others, again using the strings and the line level. You also can transfer a level line from one post to another with a water level—essentially a long hose filled with water with clear sections on each end. To transfer a level line with a water level, hold one end of the hose at the height of your reference post and line, then move the other end of the hose to the other posts. When the water level is even with your reference line and the water is the same height at the other end of the hose, mark your other posts there.

After checking again to ensure the correct heights, make the cuts with a circular saw. Again, don't cut any posts that will support railings, benches, trellises, or other built-in elements.

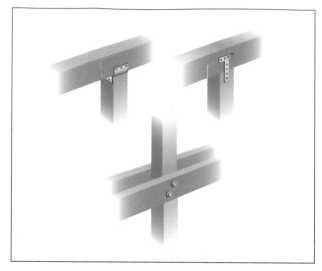

Attaching Beams

⬆ *Clockwise from top left: A post bracket holds the beam in place; if the beam isn't continuous, the break must meet above a post; beams bolted to the sides of a post allow the post to extend upward for structural support of benches, railings, or shade structures.*

Attaching the Beams

Use one of the illustrated methods, *left*, to fasten the posts and beams together. The beam most commonly sits directly on top of the post. In many cases the beams are hung from the posts using lag screws or carriage bolts, with the posts either trimmed off at the tops of the beams or extended upward to serve as deck rail supports. Joists then ride on the beams and are held in place with joist tie-downs.

Installing Cross-Bracing

Building codes often require that decks with posts taller than 6 feet have lateral bracing. Your local codes will dictate what height deck requires cross-bracing. As shown *below*, you can use wood, with diagonal, X, K, W, or Y bracing. Most bracing can be made with 2×4s, but for braces more than 8 feet long, use 2×6s. Secure braces to their posts with ⅜-inch lag screws or carriage bolts and flat washers. To prevent brace rotting and make a neater appearance, angle the end cut so that the end is vertical when the brace is installed. When two braces meet on a post, leave a small gap between them (also to prevent rot). With considerable spans and post heights, install X bracing at every bay; otherwise use it at every other bay. Never exceed a 10-foot post height without professional advice.

You might also use a gusset brace, which is a triangle made of ¾-inch exterior-grade plywood. When used at each post, the gusset works as a partial brace for decks of moderate height (5 to 7 feet). Gussets also can con-

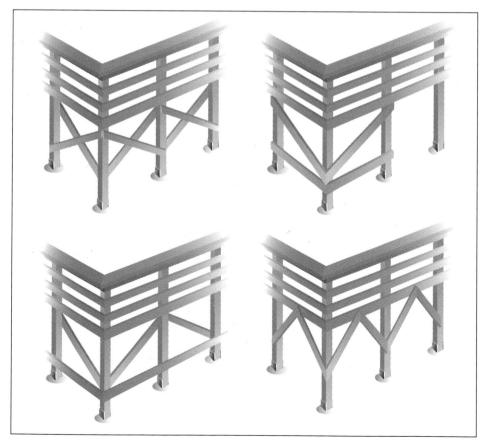

Cross-Bracing

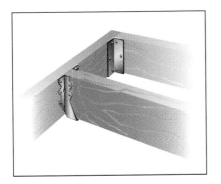

Using a Joist Hanger

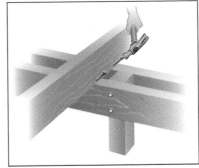

Toenailing a Joist onto a Beam

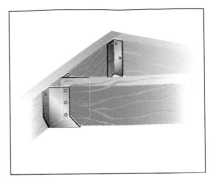

Special Slanted Joist Hangers

nect posts and beams. Fasten the gussets with closely spaced 10d (10-pennyweight) nails. Protect the top edge of the plywood from moisture by extending a member or decking over it.

Another bracing option is solid steel. Made from $3/16$- or $1/4$-inch steel angles, these pieces bolt in place and stabilize a deck by their sheer stiffness. Before installing, prime and coat metal braces with rustproof paint.

Attaching the Joists

To determine the joist lengths, start with your plan measurements but verify them on site with your tape measure. Joist hangers, *above left*, can be used to hang joists on the sides of both the ledger and the beam to achieve a more compact structural profile (especially for decks that rise only 1 or 2 feet). This configuration keeps the beams and joists on the same plane. If you use joist hangers, the tops of the joists and beam must be flush. If your joists rest on top of the beam, *above center*, you should drill pilot holes and toenail the joists to the beam, or use special brackets designed to connect two structural members perpendicular to each other.

Regardless of the method you use to secure them, start with the two joists at both ends of a deck. Set them slightly in from the deck's full width or length to allow for some overhang of the deck boards and for trim pieces, if in the plan. After you've hung the outside joists, check and adjust for square, first by using a framing square and moving the joist's outer end until it's square to the beam. Next check the diagonal measurements, as you did to square up the layout strings using the 3-4-5 method shown on page 91.

Adjust the joists until the diagonals are equal. When they are, mark the beam where the joists sit, and fasten the joists to the beam and ledger.

With the outside joists squared and fastened, install the rest of the joists at the intervals shown on your plan. Check the joist hangers and/or tie-downs to ensure all are nailed securely. This part of the job is the base for all that follows, so everything must be square, level, and securely fastened.

Solid Bridging and Tree Holes

Nail the solid bridging—intermediate joists—between the main joists wherever they span more than 2 feet. Bridging keeps the joists from twisting and helps to even out the deck load. Tree holes also need bridging for a tree that penetrates the deck platform in a place that causes a break in a joist run. Bridging used to span a break in a joist run should be twice as thick as regular bridging. This is needed because the bridging is acting as a header carrying the weight of the joist.

If your design calls for an angled or "cut" corner, it's often easiest to use special slanted joist hangers, as shown *above right*.

If your joists sit on top of the beam, nail a header board to the open ends of the joists. Some builders use fascia or skirt boards not only along the ends of the joists but also along the sides of the joists on the edge of the deck to give the deck a finished look. But if the joists along the edge of the deck look fine, there's no need to cover them.

Decking

Putting Down the Deck Surface

Use spiral- or ring-shank nails, or screws to hold down the decking (see page 38 for information about the kind of fasteners to buy). The rule of thumb for the size fastener to use is that nails should be about 2½ times as long as the thickness of the deck board and that the screws should be about twice as long. If you're using 2-inch (1½-inch-thick) boards, use 16d (16-pennyweight) nails or 3-inch-long screws.

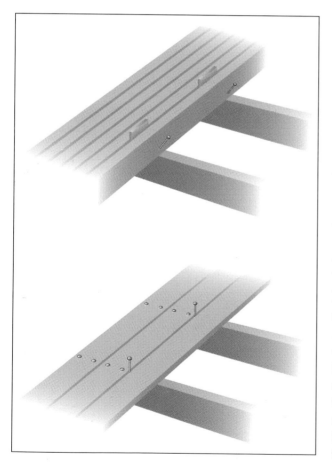

Always place fasteners at opposite edges of the board to prevent cupping, warping, and other natural tendencies of wood to distort.

Leave a ⅛- to ¼-inch space between boards so that water will drain and boards will dry off. Use wood scraps or nails, as shown in the illustration *below left*, as spacers to get consistent results. Follow the procedures in the tips below. The ends of deck boards must meet on top of a joist, with each taking up about half the thickness.

Keep the deck boards parallel with the understructure so the last board will sit evenly on the outside edge of the deck. Monitor this by measuring the distance remaining on the joists from time to time. Measure along both sides and the middle. If you discover the last board you attached is not aligned, correct the alignment of the next several deck boards gradually, adjusting the space between the next three or four boards until they're again parallel with the outside edge of the deck.

Wood-Handling Tips

■ Always nail a thinner piece of wood to a thicker piece.

■ To reduce splitting, drill a pilot hole about three-quarters of the diameter of the nail. Or, blunt the nail points by tapping them with a hammer. Blunt nails tear through wood fibers; sharp ones pry them apart.

■ Drive nails at a slight angle and toward each other for greater holding power.

■ Place nails no closer to the side edge than about half the board thickness and no closer to the end than the thickness of the board. When nailing closer to an edge, predrill the holes.

■ Remember that three small nails fasten better than a single large one.

■ Coat pressure-treated wood with water repellent after it's installed to protect against moisture.

■ Install horizontal members with a slight tilt so they drain water rather than collect it. For example, use railings that slope 5 degrees rather than dead-level ones.

Experts' Insight

Which Way Is Up?

Do you lay the boards bark side up or down? Some wood experts argue bark side down will increase the likelihood your decking will warp. If you use screws to hold down the decking, it won't warp much no matter which way you lay it down. Of more importance is the possibility of inner rings of wood separating from the board and producing a big splinter. By placing the boards bark side up, this will never happen and you can safely walk the deck with bare feet.

Design Options

The design of your decking need not be just straight across. A pattern can add visual interest to any deck just as different patterns of wood flooring add interest to a room.

Note that in all but the diagonal pattern, additional joists, or double-thick joists, are needed to allow the ends of the decking to rest firmly on the structure below.

If you do use a diagonal pattern, use the distance along the decking between joists to calculate the allowable span, not the perpendicular distance between joists.

Diagonal

Basket weave

Herringbone

Right corner

Keeping Boards Straight

Keeping deck boards straight may pose one difficulty for you. Lumber often has a slight bend that usually can be straightened as you fasten it from one end to another. More extreme bends may require some simultaneous levering and fastening, as shown *right*.

For a clean finish, cut off exposed ends of deck boards in a straight line after you've attached them to the deck, as shown *below*. If you're skilled with a circular saw, you can snap a chalk line and cut the boards off freehand. If you're not, tack a straight board in place as a guide, and keep the saw snug against it for a straight, smooth cut.

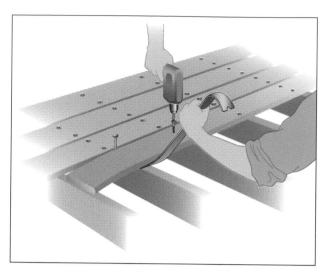

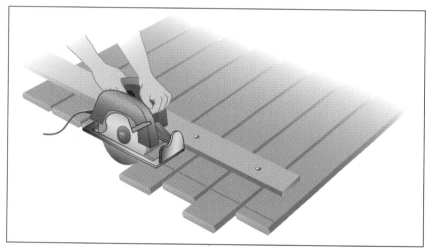

▼ *When using very long decking, it's important to keep the material parallel. With diagonal alignment, also let the tips overlap the edge of the deck, then trim them off straight.*

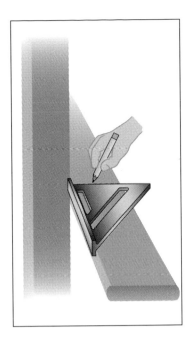

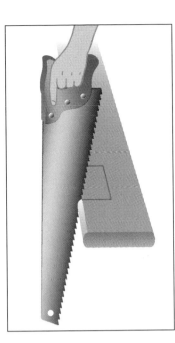

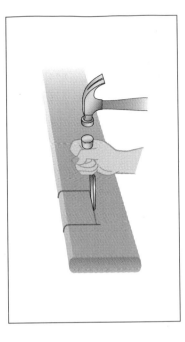

Cutting Around Notches For Posts

You may encounter areas that need to be cut or notched to fit around posts or railings. Since you haven't installed the latter yet, ignore for now any deck boards that will run into them. When you need to, mark and cut notches in the decking, as shown *above*. Line the deck up with the post and mark with a square, *above left*. Saw through the outside edges, *above center*. Use a sharp wood chisel to knock out the waste, starting a little bit away from the final cutout line and working toward it with the chisel after you've removed the majority of the waste, *above right*. You also can use a jigsaw, if you have one, for notching decking to fit around posts. If the decking needs additional support around a post, nail support blocks to the post directly under the decking.

Finishing Touches on Decking

To finish the look of your deck edges, nail on a skirt of 1-inch (¾ inch thick) lumber, but do it after attaching all railings, stairs, or other built-in structures. To avoid moisture and rotting in skirting boards, use rot-resistant redwood or cedar. If you use other wood, coat with water-resistant stain before assembly.

DESIGN DETAIL

For better looks and to avoid splinters, "break" or slightly round off sharp edges with a fine rasp, hand plane, or router with a round-over bit.

▲ *A simple skirt board hides the ends of the joists and decking and gives a finished look to the deck.*

Stairs

Do-it-yourselfers often view stair construction as difficult, but it can be simple. First decide which stringer or step support system you'll use. You can opt for open stringers that reveal tread supports or closed stringers that conceal them, as shown in the illustration *below right*. Always consider strength over style. The stringers, typically made from 2×10s or 2×12s, must carry heavy loads. For long stair runs, they may need additional post and beam support. The rise (vertical climb) and the run (horizontal dimension) of each step always should be exactly the same. If they're not, the unexpected changes in the stairway could present a tripping hazard.

Most stairs have rises of about 7 inches, with the runs ranging from 10 to 11 inches. If you prefer a gentler incline, use this rule: The sum of the run and rise should be 18 inches (perhaps a 4-inch rise with a 14-inch run). You can make gentler inclines with very deep steps of 30 to 36 inches, allowing climbers an even gait by providing enough room on each step for a full stride.

To figure the number of steps, measure the total vertical distance between the levels (labeled total rise in the illustration *below*). Divide this by 7 inches or the rise you plan to use, then round off the result to the nearest whole number. To calculate the exact rise per step, divide the total rise by the number of steps.

Next, decide the length of each step's run and multiply that by the number of steps; this represents the total run of your stairs. Check this distance at the site to ensure it's correct for the available space. You'll use the exact rise and run figures to lay out and notch the stringers.

Supporting the Treads

Now armed with the number of steps and their rises and runs, you're ready to decide how to attach the treads. If you like the appearance of open stringers, you can support the treads either by attaching cleats or making dado cuts to receive the treads. Regular or extended cleats, shown in the illustration *below*, make the job easier and preserve the stringer's full strength.

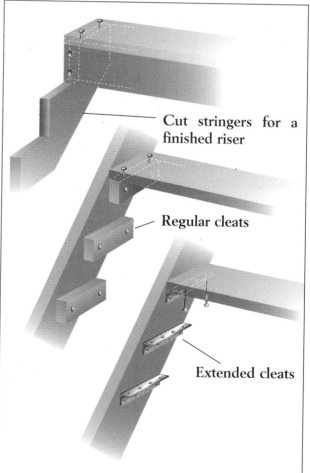

Cut stringers for a finished riser

Regular cleats

Extended cleats

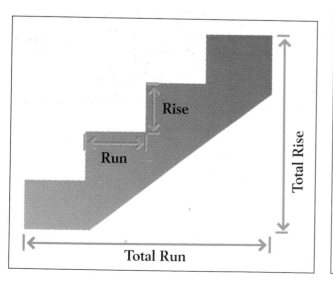

Rise

Run

Total Rise

Total Run

The easiest way to make dado cuts is with a circular saw and a dado set. The depth of the dadoes should be one-fourth to one-third of the stringer's thickness. A router also can cut dadoes neatly and is more portable.

continued

▲ *A slightly different use of common materials can produce dramatic results. Here 2×4s are turned on edge to form strong stair treads.*

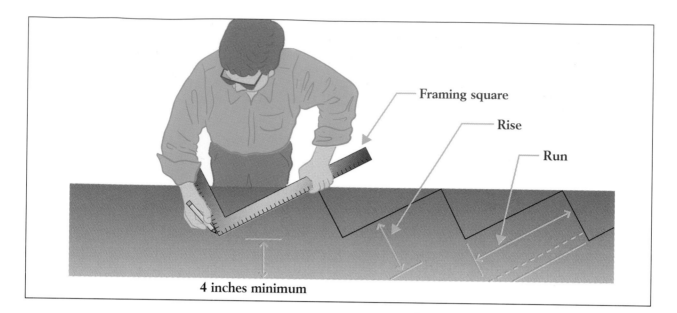

Framing square

Rise

Run

4 inches minimum

Laying Out and Cutting Open Stringers

Proper layout is critical for open stringers. On a framing square, mark the run on the long side of the board and the rise on the short side. Position the square so those marks just meet the edges of the board, as shown *above*, then pencil in the rise and the run. Reposition the square so the end of the next run exactly intersects the end of the adjacent rise; again, scribe the rise and run lines. Continue marking the stringer to the end.

The marked runs represent the location of the bottom of each tread. Because there is no tread below the first step, the riser of the first step should be shorter than all other risers by the height of the treads. To keep all steps even, saw off the thickness of one tread from the bottom of the first rise. For adequate strength in open stringers, at least 4 inches of knot-free wood should remain across the face of the stringer after you cut it.

Securing the Stringers

Safe stairs must be anchored well. Some of the easier methods include attaching the stringer to the deck using special stringer brackets, *below left*, or holding the stringer in place using a simple L-type bracket, *below center*. You also can attach a stringer by notching the stringers to ride on the deck and toenailing the stringers in place. Finish by nailing blocks to the sides of the stringers. Another viable method is to bolt the stringers to the ends of joists or headers.

The weight of a stair usually holds the stair foot in place, but you may want to attach the lower end to a footing. The illustration *below right* shows a

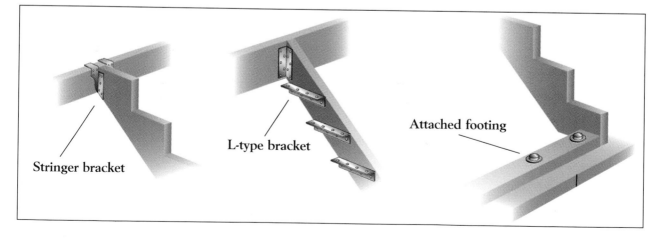

Stringer bracket

L-type bracket

Attached footing

stringer foot nailed to a board that is bolted to a concrete footing. You can achieve nearly the same stability by setting in drift pins when you pour concrete footings. Position the pins so they extend into the holes drilled in the base of each stringer.

Attaching the Treads

The way you attach your stair treads depends partly on your material. Treads usually are made from the same lumber you used for the deck boards. Most deck builders consider screws the best option for treads because you easily can remove or replace a broken or worn tread.

With open stringers and closed stringers with cleats, you must drive screws down in the face of the treads. Drill pilot holes to prevent splitting. With closed stringers that have dadoes, the screws can be driven through the side of the stringer and into the tread ends.

Adding a Stair Rail

Stair rails safeguard against accidents. Even a short stair should have one. The typical height of the rail is 30 to 40 inches. The key members of a stair rail are the posts. You may include balusters between the posts, as shown *above right*, or you may go for a more open look.

If you plan to use a 2×4 top rail, keep the span between posts at less than 6 feet. For 2×6 or larger rails, you can use spans of up to 8 feet. Attach the posts to the stringers or to the deck

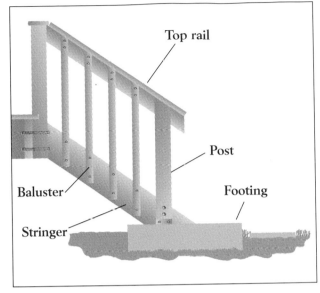

framing with bolts or lag screws. Your building code may contain minimum requirements for stair rails. As long as they're safe and practical, try to style this element after your deck railing.

Alternative Access: Building a Ramp

If you need wheelchair access between the house, deck, or yard, you can substitute a ramp for stairs as shown *below*. The main difference between a wheelchair ramp and stairs is that the ramp angle must be much shallower, so that it isn't a struggle. Most code requirements limit the rise-to-run ratio to 1 to 8. (For example, a 2-foot rise must be spread out over a 16-foot run.)

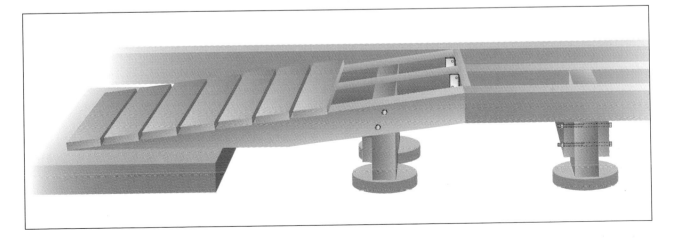

Door Installation

Because most exterior walls bear the weight of upper floors and roof framing, you must devise a temporary support system to carry the load while you modify the walls. The precise steps may vary depending on whether you buy a hinged or sliding door and if the door has preattached molding. Regardless, the general steps below should guide you through the process.

If your new doorway will replace a window, you can remove the old unit, sash and all. Wait

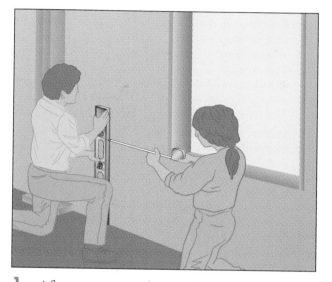

1. After removing the window, use the rough opening as a reference point to mark the opening for the door on the inside and outside of the wall. Use a level to make vertical lines.

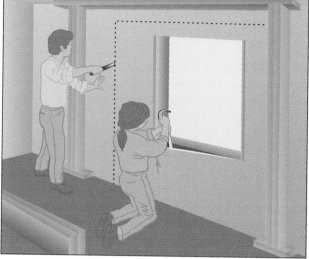

2. Set up the bracing. You'll need one person to hold a 2×4 against the ceiling while you wedge in the vertical members. Pull away the interior wall using a crow bar or hammer.

3. Cut the siding and sheathing with a circular saw set at a depth of the siding's thickness. Be careful not to cut into any wiring. When you get to the floor, saw through the 2×4 sole plate, too.

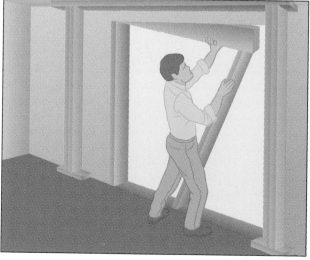

4. Use jack studs to wedge the header in place, nail the jack studs to the king studs, and toenail the header into position. Add cripple studs between the header and top plate if needed.

until you expose the studs on both sides, then pry them away from the window frame. Cut through the exterior of the house in good weather, and be sure to have someone help you lift the header into position. Always work from the inside out, cutting the exterior sheathing and siding just before you insert the sliding door. Once you have installed the door, patch and paint the inte-

rior wall. Nail the desired trim or molding around the new door.

A brick wall opening calls for substantially more work. It requires a masonry saw for cutting through brick and requires installing an angle iron or metal I-beam lintel to support the bricks above the door. Consult a professional builder for a brick wall opening.

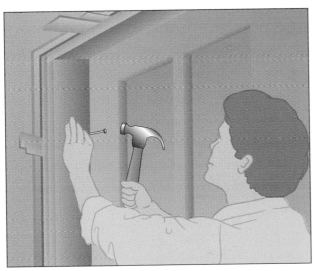

5. If your door has preattached brick molding, position the door in place, making sure it is level and plumb. Trace a line around the brick molding onto the siding.

6. Cut through the siding but not the sheathing below. Insert 8-inch-wide strips of building paper between the siding and the sheathing. Bend them around the framing and staple them in place.

7. Reinsert the jamb. Level and plumb the frame by inserting shims where required, and nail or screw through the shims. Trim off the shims and insulate between the jamb and the framing.

8. If your door didn't come with preattached molding, bridge the gap between the frame and siding by nailing up molding. Seal between the molding and house with paintable silicone caulk.

Stain and Protection

Even the best-built decks can't escape weathering. For protection, use coatings to preserve the wood's natural color. To get the color you want, perhaps to match your house, use exterior stains.

Coat the decking material with a clear wood finish soon after you complete the deck, then do so annually. Do not let nature take its course if you want a weathered look; varying amounts of exposure produce different appearances in different places. Get a more even weathered look with an exterior stain in one of numerous shades of gray from several manufacturers.

What Type of Stain?

Penetrating stains come in three types: transparent, semitransparent, and opaque. Transparent stains have no pigments but do have water-repellent features that protect the wood without hiding its natural coloration. Semitransparent stains modify the original wood color but don't rob the wood of its natural qualities. Semitransparent stains are much more durable than transparent stains. High in pigment content, opaque stains thoroughly hide the wood grain and color.

First be sure that all surfaces are clean, dry, and free of mildew, dirt, dust, oil, soot, and other contaminants. These contaminants can be removed by washing with a solution of 1 quart bleach, 3 quarts water, and 1 cup of a nonammoniated detergent. Thoroughly rinse and dry the deck after washing.

Deck stains or coatings give maximum performance when the wood has dried to a moisture content below 20 percent. Deck materials often have a high moisture content when purchased, but even if the wood feels wet, it's important to apply a coating to protect it from the sun. Only the wood surface must be dry. If the surface you want to stain soaks up a few drops of water, it's dry enough to stain.

Use bristle brushes to apply stain or repellent. To prevent lap marks, apply only one coat on smooth or rough woods. Always apply by overlapping wet areas. Allowing an area to dry and then overlapping it with wet stain may produce inconsistent color. You can use rollers or a sprayer to apply stain quickly, but use a brush to work the stain into the wood.

If you prefer a painted look, buy an opaque stain or an exterior latex- or alkyd-based paint. Apply these only to redwood, cedar, or pressure-treated lumber after the wood becomes sufficiently dry. This may take from one to six months. If coatings must be applied to unseasoned wood before this time, use a water-based product over a stain-blocking latex primer formulated for these woods.

A final word of caution: Do not use clear, film-forming varnishes such as urethane, polyurethane, or spar varnish; lacquers; or shake-and-shingle coatings on exterior deck surfaces.

Maintenance

Maintain your deck regularly, keeping it swept of dirt and leaves. Once a year, inspect the deck for any loose connectors. Drive in any popped nails, and tighten screws and through-bolts.

Moisture penetrates wood year-round, especially at board ends and joints, where rot will occur. Apply a wood preservative annually to all spots that are prone to rotting.

In addition to water, normal wear can take its toll, especially on rails, stair treads, and stringers. If any of these feel spongy or if cracks appear, replace them immediately.

PROBLEM ? SOLUTION

Stains on the Deck

Stains from many sources can mar the look of your deck. Your first line of defense is with a deck sealer or exterior color stain, which will resist unwanted staining. To combat mold and mildew stains, scrub with a mixture of water and household bleach, or use a commercial mildew killer.

Remove such common food stains as barbecue sauce and grease with a water-rinsable automotive degreaser. Don't apply these removers when the surface is exposed to direct sun; apply these only in shade.

Leaf stains are black and oily, so if they penetrate the existing protective coating, treat the stains with household bleach mixed with an equal amount of water. For extreme cases, use bleach full strength. If your bleach is too strong and lightens the wood too much, use a clear wood finish or a stain to bring back the color.

Difficult green stains almost always reappear because the algae and moss that cause them form a root structure in the wood. Control these by applying full-strength bleach and a deck restorer, and vigorously scrubbing.

Rust from nails, furniture, or toys will form brown or black spots. Use a 5-percent solution of oxalic acid in water and apply it, twice, directly to the stain. Remember to rinse the area well before applying a wood sealer.

Building Steps

Although there may be a dizzying number of things to keep track of when building a deck, the process can be outlined quickly (see below). Step number one, believe it or not, may take as long as all the subsequent steps combined, except for the last one. Spend enough time on the first step and the rest should be much easier.

1 Have your permit, plans, tools, and materials ready to go
2 Prepare the site
3 Stake the perimeter and the footings
4 Dig post footings
5 Secure the posts
6 Mix and pour concrete
7 Set the post connectors
8 Set the posts
9 Attach the ledger board
10 Cut the posts to height
11 Attach the beams
12 Install cross-bracing
13 Set the joists
14 Lay the deck boards
15 Nail the deck surface
16 Put finishing touches on the decking
17 Build the stairs
18 Support the stair treads
19 Lay out and cut open stringers
20 Secure the stringers
21 Attach the treads
22 Build a stair rail
23 Attach the railing to the deck
24 Stain and protect deck if needed
25 ENJOY!

Glossary

Actual Dimensions. The exact measurements of a piece of lumber. For instance, a 2×4 (nominal dimensions) is actually 1½ inches thick by 3½ inches wide.

Attached Deck. A deck with one or more sides supported by a ledger and attached to a house.

Baluster. One of a series of vertical supports used between posts of a railing. Also called a spindle.

Beam. A horizontal support member on which joists rest. Beams usually are supported by posts.

Bevel Gauge. Also known as a T-bevel, the bevel gauge is a flat piece of metal attached to a handle with a wing nut that allows the metal piece to be set at any angle to the handle. It's used primarily to mark angles when copying them from a plan or piece of the deck to another piece.

Block Plane. A small plane used to finish off rough edges of a deck.

Bracing. Structural supports placed between posts and beams or joists to provide stability to the structure.

Bridging. Boards placed perpendicularly between joists to stiffen the joists. Frequently, bridging is made from the same dimension lumber as the joists.

Buglehead Screw. A screw with a curved taper between the head and shank or threads so it doesn't tear the wood when screwed down flush with the surface.

Cap Rail. The top horizontal piece of a railing, usually placed to give it a finished appearance.

Carriage Bolt. A bolt with a rounded head that is pulled down onto the surface of the wood as the nut is tightened. Used to hold structural members together, the rounded head gives a finished look to the bolt. Bolts should be checked annually and tightened if necessary.

Cement. A powder that serves as a binding element in concrete and mortar. Also, any adhesive.

Chalk Line. An enclosed reel of string coated with colored chalk and used to mark straight lines by pulling the string taut and snapping the string, leaving a line of chalk marking a line. Commonly used in deck building to mark the edge of decking so that all decking boards can be cut off flush with each other.

Codes. Regulations detailing accepted materials and methods of building. Usually codes are adopted by city, county, or state building departments. Most counties promulgate local building codes.

Concrete. A mixture of cement, sand, and gravel.

Concrete Spatula. A flat piece of metal with a projecting handle used to smooth concrete footings.

Conduit. Metal pipes used to contain electrical wiring in outdoor settings.

Decking. Boards used for the surface of a deck.

Easement. A legal right for restricted use of property by the easement holder. Easements often are granted to utility companies so they may service the utility lines running through a property. Decks should not be built on the area described by an easement because access granted by the easement may require the deck be torn down or removed.

Elevated Deck. A deck requiring a structure of footings, posts, and beams to raise it to the desired level. Often used so that the height of the deck is the same as interior floors, making access to the deck from the house easier.

Flat-Sawn Boards. See Plain-Sawn Boards.

Footing. The below-ground support of a deck's post, usually made from concrete.

Framing Square. A flat piece of metal shaped like an L, with measurements along both legs of the L, commonly used when building decks for marking lines perpendicular to the length of lumber.

Freestanding Platform Deck. A deck supported entirely by its own structure, typically used for remote decks.

Galvanize. Coating a piece of metal with zinc, a metal that resists corrosion. Look for hot-dipped galvanized pieces when selecting metal parts for a deck. The hot-dipped method of galvanizing metal provides more protection than coated galvanizing.

GFCI. See Ground-Fault Circuit Interrupter.

Grade. A designation given to lumber indicating the amount of flaws and knots typically found in the wood. Most builders recommend using #1 grade wood for building decks. Also, the surface of the ground.

Grade-Level Deck. A deck flush with, or slightly above, ground level. Grade-level deck joists usually rest directly on the footings or piers below.

Ground-Fault Circuit Interrupter (GFCI). An electrical safety device that instantly shuts down a circuit if leakage occurs, greatly reducing the risk of electrical shock. These devices commonly are built into outlets and usually are required by code for outdoor receptacles.

Incised Wood. Wood with slots cut into the side of the wood so that preservative chemicals can penetrate more deeply during pressure treatment. Western species of wood don't absorb preservative chemicals as easily as some woods and require incising so that enough of the preservative enters the wood.

Joist. Horizontal framing members that support decking.

Joist Hanger. A premanufactured metal piece typically attached to a ledger or beam to support a joist. Joist hangers should be galvanized.

Lag Screw. A large screw, usually 4 inches or longer, with a hex head, turned with a wrench.

Lattice. A framework of crossed wood made of laths or other thin pieces of wood. Lattice often can be bought premade in 4×8 sheets.

Ledger. A length of board, usually a 2×8 or 2×10, that is horizontally attached to the side of a house and holds up one edge of a deck.

Linear Feet. The total length of required lumber. For example, three 8-foot-long 2×4s and four 6-foot-long 2×4s both would be described as 24 linear feet of 2×4s.

Line Level. A level that hangs from a mason's line, typically used to transfer level elevations from one post to another.

Live Load. The amount of weight a deck is designed to support. Most deck designs call for a live load of 60 pounds per square foot.

Load Area. The area found by multiplying the beam spacing by the post spacing to determine the post thickness required by building codes.

Low-Voltage Lighting. Commercially available lighting systems that use a transformer to reduce the needed electrical current. These lighting systems are designed for do-it-yourself applications.

Machine Bolt. A bolt typically configured with a hex head and nut and a blunt end. Meant to hold two pieces (usually the support structure) by pinning them together, the threads hold only the nut and don't screw into the wood itself.

Mason's Line. String that does not stretch, making it useful to establish horizontal lines when laying out the various heights of a deck.

Multilevel Deck. A deck that has several discrete areas at different levels. The different levels often are built to conform to a sloping terrain or make a transition from a second story to ground level.

Nail Set. A short shaft of metal with a narrow blunt point used to set nail heads below the surface of wood by placing the blunt end on the nail head and striking the other end with a hammer.

Nominal Dimensions. The label given to a standard piece of lumber. For example, 2×4 is the name for a rough-cut piece of about 2×4 inches. It is then finished by planing and sometimes sanding it down to its actual dimensions.

On Center. A method of measuring distance between two structural members, such as joists, where you measure from the center of one member to the center of the other. Abbreviated O.C.

Pennyweight. A system of measuring the size of a nail. Originally derived from a unit of weight, pennyweight is represented by the letter "d."

Pier. A masonry post. Piers often serve as above-grade footings for posts and often are made of precast concrete.

Plain-Sawn Boards. Boards sawn from a log so that the face of the board is at an angle less than 30 degrees to the growth rings in the log. Sometimes referred to as flat-sawn boards. See also Quartersawn Boards and Rift-Sawn Boards.

Plastic Wood. Wood made from sawdust and recycled plastic so that it resembles and can be cut like actual wood. Not suitable for structural support, it is made primarily for use as decking. One popular brand is called Trex.

Plumb Bob. A weight designed to hang from a string to mark a vertical line. Plumb bobs are used to locate the exact position of a footing or post anchor below a deck's designated layout.

Post. The vertical structural element that rests on the footing and supports the beam.

Post Anchor. A metal piece attached to or imbedded in the footing that attaches the post to the footing and keeps the post from being exposed to moisture in the ground.

Post Cap. A small piece of wood attached to the top of the post to cover the post's wood grain and protect the post from the weather.

Pressure-Treated Wood. Wood subjected to a high-pressure treatment of chemicals as a preservative. The most common chemical used for treatment is chromated copper arsenate (CCA). Sometimes known as green wood because of the residual color of the chemical.

Quartersawn Boards. Boards sawn from a log so that the face of the board is at an angle between 60 degrees and 90 degrees to the growth rings in the log. Quartersawn boards generally are more stable and warp less than plain-sawn and rift-sawn boards.

Rail Post. A vertical structural support for the railing, sometimes also supporting the deck itself and extending down to a footing. Rail posts usually are thicker than balusters and are attached with bolts to the joists or beams.

Remote Deck. A freestanding platform located away from the house, typically placed for a good view.

Rift-Sawn Boards. Boards sawn from a log so that the face of the board is at an angle between 30 degrees and 60 degrees to the growth rings in the log. See also Quartersawn Boards and Plain-Sawn Boards.

Ring-Shank Nail. A nail with grooves and ridges around the shank to prevent the nail from popping out of the wood as the wood contracts and expands because of changes in moisture and temperature.

Rise. The vertical distance from one stair tread to another.

Riser. The vertical piece between two stair steps.

Run. The horizontal distance from one stair riser to another or the depth of a stair step.

Setback. The area along a property's edge where new construction is restricted or forbidden by local zoning laws.

Shade Structure. A structure built above decks, usually of posts and lattice, to provide a shaded area on the deck.

Skirt. A decorative board placed around the support structure of a deck to hide the structure below and give the deck a finished appearance. Skirts often are attached to the joists.

Span. The distance between supports.

Spindle. See Baluster.

Spiral-Shank Nail. A nail with helical grooves and ridges around the shank to prevent the nail from popping out of the wood as the wood contracts and expands because of changes in moisture and temperature. This nail looks as if it has been twisted along its axis.

Thumbnail. A small rough sketch of the deck and its site.

Torpedo Level. A short level used in deck building to set posts plumb. It is sometimes referred to as a canoe level.

Tread. The horizontal piece of a stair step.

Trellis. A framework of thin lumber designed to support climbing plants.

Water Level. A hose or tube filled with water, used in deck construction to transfer elevations from one post to another. The surface of the water at both ends of the hose must come to rest at the same height, allowing transfer of elevations.

Zoning Laws. Laws adopted by local governments that restrict the location and type of new construction.

Index

Numbers in **bold** typeface indicate pages where the item listed is photographed.

U.S. Units to Metric Equivalents		
To convert from	Multiply by	To get
Inches	25.4	Millimeters (mm)
Inches	2.54	Centimeters (cm)
Feet	30.48	Centimeters (cm)
Feet	0.3048	Meters (m)
Cubic Feet	28.316	Liters (l)

Metric Units to U.S. Equivalents		
To convert from	Multiply by	To get
Millimeters	0.0394	Inches
Centimeters	0.3937	Inches
Centimeters	0.0328	Feet
Meters	3.2808	Feet
Liters	0.0353	Cubic Feet